Proceeds from Internet-Electronic Sales of this book will
be used to underwrite the ministry of
Published By Parables
We publish Christian Books -- FREE

If you've written a Christian book
or a book about Jesus or the Christian life -- Contact Us
www.PublishedByParables.com

Proceeds from off-line Sales generated by Contributing
Authors can be used by the Authors to support their
ministries, other ministries or in whatever
way they deem appropriate.

Tell Someone About This Book
Share It With Someone Who Has Need

Broken Beyond Belief -- But Not Beyond Faith

VOLUME 1

Compiled and Written By...
DR. JOHN DEE JEFFRIES
EDITED BY C. GENEVIEVE JEFFRIES
Author of The Last Martyr; When I Can't Find God;
Hip. Hip. Hallelujah! Book 1, 2 & 3 and
To The Shepherds of the New Millennium

PUBLISHED *by* PARABLES
Earthly Stories with a Heavenly Meaning

Broken Beyond Belief -- But Not Beyond Faith
Compiled and Written By...
DR. JOHN DEE JEFFRIES
EDITED BY C. GENEVIEVE JEFFRIES
Author of The Last Martyr; When I Can't Find God; Hip. Hip. Hallelujah! Book 1, 2 & 3 and To The Shepherds.
.

Copyright © John Dee Jeffries
December, 2017

Published By Parables
December, 2017

Cover Design by Fury Cover Design / www.furycoverdesign.com

All Rights Reserved. No part of this book may be reproduced or utilized in any form or by any means, electronic or mechanical, including photocopying, recording, or by any information storage and retrieval system, without permission in writing from the author.

Unless otherwise specified Scripture quotations are taken from the authorized version of the King James Bible.

    ISBN 978-1-945698-40-8
    Printed in the United States of America

Readers should be aware that Internet Web sites offered as citations and/or sources for further information may have been changed or disappeared between the time this was written and when it is read.

Broken Beyond Belief -- But Not Beyond Faith

VOLUME 1

Compiled and Written By...
DR. JOHN DEE JEFFRIES
EDITED BY C. GENEVIEVE JEFFRIES
Author of The Last Martyr; When I Can't Find God;
Hip. Hip. Hallelujah! Book 1, 2 & 3 and
To The Shepherds of the New Millennium

PUBLISHED *by* PARABLES
Earthly Stories with a Heavenly Meaning

Published By Parables
We Publish Christian Books -- FREE

OUR MISSION

The primary mission of *Published By Parables*, a Christian publisher, is to publish Contemporary and Classic Christian books from an evangelical perspective that honors Christ and promotes the values and virtues of His Kingdom.

Are You An Aspiring Christian Author?

We fulfill our mission best by providing Christian authors and writers publishing options that are uniquely Christian, quick and easy to understand -- in an effort to please Christ who has called us to a writing-publishing ministry. We know the challenges of getting published, especially if you're a first-time author. God, who called you to write your book, will provide the grace sufficient to the task of getting it published.

We understand the value of a dollar; know the importance of producing a quality product; and publish what we publish for the glory of God.

Surf and Explore our site --
then use our easy-to-use "Tell Us" button
to tell us about yourself and about your book.

We're a one-stop, full-service Christian publisher.
We know our limits. We know our capabilities.
You won't be disappointed.

www.PublishedByParables.com
Dr. John Dee Jeffries
504-715-1479

DEDICATION

To Those Who Suffer
And To Those Who Strive
To Find God's Purpose and Pathway Through Their Pain
May They Find Christ Their Very Present Help

Proceeds from internet and online sales of
Broken Beyond Belief -- But Not Beyond Faith
are used to underwrite the ministry of
Published By Parables

We publish Christian Books -- FREE

Table of Contents

Introduction	Stuff Happens *Life in a fallen world*		p.5
Chapter 1	The Serenity Prayer *God, Grant Me The Serenity...*		p.8
Chapter 2	The Reality Prayer *Lord Help Me To See...*		p.11
Chapter 3	Wesley Harville *Standing Up On The Inside*		p.13
Chapter 4	Kathryn Smith *God is Faithful, No Matter What*		p.23
Chapter 5	John Dee Jeffries *Wounded Women – Sad Sex*		p.35
Chapter 6	Martina Gallegos *The Night My Life Began*		p.43
Chapter 7	Jane Daly *The Greatest Loss*		p.57
Chapter 8	Lisa Denny *The Making Of A Jewel*		p.65
Chapter 9	Rev. John P. Harris *When Dreams Are Dashed*		p.75
Chapter 10	John Dee Jeffries *A Dark Companion Defeated*		p.93
Chapter 11	Myra Jean Myers *'Oh GOD, I Have Murdered!'*		p.101
Chapter 12	Brenda Stephens *Dark Winter's Night*		p.107

Chapter 13	Dr. Jonathan Powell *But God Is Still Working*	p.115
Chapter 14	Deborah Taylor *My Three Crosses*	p.127
Chapter 15	Terry Martin *The Girl from Phonexville*	p.137
Chapter 16	Julie Gossack *Julie's Cancer Story*	p.147
Chapter 17	Mary J. Wagner *Burned Beyond Belief*	p.159
Chapter 18	Anthony Ritthaler *Escaping Depression*	p.169
Chapter 19	Donna Britt *I Can Dance*	p.181
Chapter 20	Anna K. Schmidt *Looking For the Light*	p.193
Chapter 21	Carol Graham *Return the child. Give him back*	p.205
Chapter 22	Joy Wright Yarborough *The Wounds Of Love*	p.217
Chapter 23	John Dee Jeffries *Chicken*	p.233
Chapter 24	*Certitude*	p.235

BROKEN BEYOND BELIEF -- BUT NOT BEYOND FAITH

Introduction
Stuff Happens

Stuff happens. Good stuff and not so good stuff. Bad things happen too -- to bad people, to good people, to God's people, to all people. Bad stuff – it's the stuff of life in a fallen world…and it happens.

We may wish that bad stuff wouldn't happen – but it does. We may wish that bad stuff would go away – but it won't. Some may say it doesn't exist – but we know that it does. So, we live with it. It's all around us – it happens.

Sometimes, however, life and its bad stuff spins out of control. Sometimes the bad stuff is not just "out there" —it's close, too close. It's knocking at our door, or the door of someone we love. Our life suddenly becomes chaotic, confusing and complicated.

Life itself is complicated, complicated by its very nature, because people are complicated. Caught in the complications of life, as bad stuff happens, we suddenly find ourselves in the thick of trouble. Bad stuff is troubling. Our life or the life of someone we love, is suddenly spinning out of control. We find ourselves caught in a dark downward spiral. We come face to face with our mortality, our powerlessness, our inability and our human frailty. Life becomes unmanageable as things spin more and more out of control.

We work hard to end the madness and we struggle to straighten things out. Nothing happens. We work hard to right our sinking ship. Still, nothing happens. Finally, we throw up our hands in frustration, defeat, desperation and despair -- and we give up. We're broken – *Broken Beyond Belief – But Not Beyond Faith.*

This book is not intended to be a how-to book, or a 10-steps-to-greatness book. This is an honest, raw and vulnerable collection of true stories written by salt-of-the-earth people who bounced back from the bottom -- by the power of Jesus Christ. Their testimony? It's simple and straightforward: Christ has come to heal the brokenhearted. Because of His grace and providence, no one is so badly broken that they are broken beyond faith.

It's hard to yield to God's leadership when life is broken and spinning out of control; but, it's the only way to find peace and serenity.

We may not always know or understand God's plan – but we can have peace and serenity. There really is a calm in the middle of the storm.

So, let's make a deal. Since today really is the first day of the rest of your life – let's live like it. Here's the deal. <u>Let's live today and the days that follow with eager anticipation.</u> Deal? Okay? Thanks for making the deal. Now...

Like a runner at the starting block you are probably filled with eager anticipation (Remember our deal? Look at that underlined sentence. Remember our deal).

Okay. Let's start again…It is day one! A new journey has just begun and you're off and running. Be assured, the race you are now running is laden with unspeakable opportunity -- and challenges. Blessings multiplied await the diligent. You're on a faith journey, running with patience the race that is before you (Hebrews 12:1).

Beside you, with you, and for you is a "friend who sticks closer than a brother" (Proverbs 18:24). Jesus is that Friend. He will guide you through this journey to delightful shores which yesterday seemed a distant dream. In the running of this race you are not alone. Jesus is running patiently with you, beside you, blazing a new trail for you – because He loves and cares for you.

So run, but do not rush nor be frantic in your efforts. So many feel they are not making progress unless they are swiftly, speedily, and frantically forging head.

Remember, a falling star races through the evening sky, burns brightly, yet with it's great haste proceeds to burn itself out -- to its own destruction!

Today is the day you put your hand to the plow. New furrows are being prepared within your heart by the Holy Spirit to enable you to receive the good seed of the Word of God. Remember, however, that the fruit of our labor ripens slowly. So, be patient. In the running of this race the diligent reap an abundant harvest through patience.

Haste, like a strangling weed, will choke the good seed that is to be sown and imprison your future. There are no short-cuts, nor are there quick solutions. He who is beside you, with you and for you is in no hurry!

So run, but with patience, and pray that you will yield to the wisdom of His guidance and the loving direction of His Spirit.

THE SERENITY PRAYER

Long ago an American theologian, Reinhold Neibuhr (1892-1971), wrote the Serenity Prayer, one of the most popular prayers ever written. The prayer was originally used in sermons, Bible study classes and Sunday school groups. Alcoholics Anonymous began to use a shortened version of the Serenity Prayer in their twelve step program in the early 40s.

"God grant me the serenity to accept the things I cannot change; courage to change the things I can; and the wisdom to know the difference."

The Serenity Prayer is helpful in both one-on-one and/or group counseling sessions. I often give the following written assignment when using the Serenity Prayer in counseling situations:

(1) write the Serenity Prayer, a word at a time or a phrase at a time, and analyze each word and phrase,

(2) clarify and explain in simple terms the meaning of the individual words and phrases in the prayer; and,

(3) spell out any life principals that you see in the prayer.

After the assignment is completed I offer the following thoughts for consideration.

> Serenity is the opposite of frustration, anxiety and fear.
>
> Serenity is not something we crank up. It's granted as a gift given from God.
>
> Even though serenity is a gift that is given by God, it is also a goal that must be gained.
>
> Even though the goal must be gained, it is still, nevertheless, a gift that must be accepted, received by faith.

At the base of this prayer and its principled process is a cooperative ministry, a cooperative ministry between us and God. In that cooperative relationship there is a part that is God's that we cannot do (God will do His part) and there is a part that is ours that God will not do (We must do our part).

As God does what only God can do we make a humbling yet awesome discovery -- there are some things that we can and some things that we cannot change.

We cannot change other <u>people</u>. We cannot change

the <u>past</u> and we cannot change the reality of the <u>pain</u> that we experienced at certain <u>places</u> where unpleasant events happened.

Because this process is so delicate and difficult, God grants us the necessary courage to change the only thing that we really can change – ourselves from pain.

We often waste valuable time and energy trying to change others or we try to deconstruct the past or we deploy other defense mechanisms to protect ourselves.

Sometimes we take the opposite approach and acquiesce. We give up. We ignore or stuff the pain or we cower in fear, falsely believing that we are powerless and helpless. These inadequate approaches reveal a lack of emotional strength and courage to change the only thing we can change – ourselves…and so we languish in our brokenness.

Good News. Through Jesus Christ, your Lord and Savior, you have the power of the Holy Spirit available to you. The Holy Spirit will give you the serenity, the courage and the wisdom you need to follow and fulfill God's plan for your life.

Instead of anxiously ignoring tough decisions or running from difficult choices, we can call upon the power of God for courage and wisdom to move forward even in the midst of great adversity.

Wisdom is a gift given by God to those who ask for it! Serenity, courage and wisdom are gained as you spend time reading the Bible and talking with God through prayer.

So hold on to your dreams. Hold on to your hope. Don't give up. Don't turn back. Continue to *run with patience the race that is before you.*

The Reality Prayer

The Wounded Healer is the title of a brief biography of the late J. B. Phillips, a prominent theologian/Bible translator. In the midst of his life story the biographer included a copy of a prayer that Phillips had prayed.

Years ago as I read that particular prayer the Holy Spirit pierced my heart. He literally gripped me, seized my attention and led me to claim that prayer, pray that prayer and make it my own.

I have prayed and do pray that prayer often with the conviction that its answer in my life and in the lives of all of God's children is one of the great needs of the hour. I choose to call that prayer, though J. B. Phillips did not label it such, "The Reality Prayer." It is a very short, very concise, very simple prayer and I pray that the Holy Spirit will use it in your life as you follow Jesus:

> *"God, Help me to see the world as it is; myself as I am; and, Thou as Thou art."*

I really believe that God is genuinely pleased when His people pray that kind of prayer. It is a prayer for truth; a simple request for the ability to understand; for discernment; for wisdom; for the gift of seeing reality unencumbered by the many illusions that distort our perceptions, cloud our understanding and hinder us in our pilgrimage through this world.

It is a prayer to see in three directions: Upward (God), Inward (Self) and Outward (World). Pray that prayer and pray it often. God will hear and He will bless you.

God will never leave you, nor forsake you
Especially in your hour of need
Especially in your brokenness

Wesley Harville
Standing Up On The Inside

"I have no use of my legs, my lung muscles are weak which greatly limits my speaking abilities and my arms and hands are almost useless. I cannot use a standard keyboard or phone. I am typing this with eye recognition technology. Yes sir, I am typing this email with my eye."

--- Commentary / John Dee Jeffries ---

The writer of the email was Wesley Harville, a disabled pastor in Arkansas afflicted with ALS. The email was sent to me, Dr. John Dee Jeffries, CEO/Acquisitions Editor, *Published By Parables* and long-term pastor of First Baptist Church, Chalmette, Louisiana.

"I have no use of my legs, my lung muscles are weak which greatly limits my speaking abilities and my arms and hands are almost useless. I cannot use a standard keyboard or phone. I am typing this with eye recognition technology. Yes sir, I am typing this email with my eye."

Physically, Wesley Harville may be knocked down but spiritually he's standing up on the inside as he continues to run with patience (bearing under the load) the race that is set is before him.

"I am a retired Baptist pastor," related Harville. "I have served as pastor of God's churches in Arkansas and Illinois for thirty years with the belief that I could never retire from doing what I loved most, preaching the Good News of Jesus Christ."

Harville saw each day as an opportunity to proclaim Christ. Then one day adversity came, severe adversity, hard times.

"I have learned that my ways are not always His ways," says Harville.

At the onset of Harville's ministry there were no real dark days, other than the everyday, run-of-the-mill tough times that we all deal with on occasion. No. Life back then was filled with eager anticipation. God had called Wesley into the ministry. Wesley responded to that call – and enrolled in seminary. It was evident that Wesley was an evangelistic, soul-winning, mission-minded Gospel preacher. He loved God, loved the people of God, loved the Word of God – and he loved the lost.

"In 1979 I met a student at the Missionary Baptist Seminary in Little Rock, Arkansas, who would prove to be a lifelong friend and fellow servant of the Lord Jesus Christ," shared Rev. Mark T. Thornton. "We shared classes together throughout our seminary days. It didn't take long to see that Wesley was serious about serving the Lord. He became a dedicated missionary, a loving pastor, and a faithful family man, not necessarily in that order."

In life, if you look closely, you'll see that there are many people who share life with us during our life journey. It was no different for Wesley. (It's no different for any of us). Look again, closely, and you'll also see that there are also some extra special people who not only share our journey but shape us in ways that are deep and profound!

Rev. Paul Goodwin was one such man. He was a shaper of men, especially of young ministers and he had a powerful influence on young Wesley. Goodwin's evangelism class caused Wesley to see how a specific method of memorizing Scripture could help someone hide God's Word in their heart. Wesley embraced that method – but he wasn't alone.

It seems to be woven into the fabric of life that each of us have people, like Paul Goodwin, placed nearby by God to help and influence us. Goodwin did indeed have a strong influence on Wesley; but, no one had a stronger influence on Wesley than Wesley's wife, Sherrie. Wesley and Sherrie prayed together, ministered together, studied together and began to memorize God's Word together. They enhanced Goodwin's method, built upon it and developed a more effective way to memorize Scripture, a way that worked, nor only for them, but for others too.

Life was good. Graduation. Ministry. A family. Day after day the Harville's gave their very best to the cause of Christ. Wesley stood before God on behalf of the people and he stood before the people on behalf of God. The young couple would share the love of God, and share that love some more. They would give their all, and then give some more. Day after day they poured out their lives for God and for the people He entrusted into their care.

God's eternal master plan seemed to be unfolding.

Days became weeks. Weeks became months. Months became years....the decades rolled on, time passed.

"Teach us to number our days, that we may apply our hearts unto wisdom..." (Psalm 90:12)

Nothing happens by accident is a slogan that has worked its way into popular usage in American culture. The steps of the righteous are ordered by the Lord, says the psalmist (Psalm 37:23). To every thing there is a season, and a time to every purpose under the heaven (Ecclesiastes 3:3). For the great majority of us everything in life seems to happen the way it's supposed to happen. We live. We love. We watch life unfold. And we learn that there is much in life that we can and much in life that we cannot control.

Wisdom tells us that it is impossible to live in this world without ever facing adversity. Faith enables us to see, however, that no matter what is going on around us we can continue moving forward.

Today, Wesley is very much alive, still moving forward, living in the present moment, fully engaged in life -- physically immobilized, yet moving forward, fighting the good fight of faith. He is afflicted with ALS, a terminal illness. He has his diagnosis. He knows his prognosis. Nevertheless, Wesley is still weathering the storm, still moving forward.

Shortly after receiving his diagnosis Sherrie died. And now he must daily endure the ravages of ALS without her by his side. Her absence may be more painful than ALS.

Inward battles with uncertainty, doubt, confusion, fear and more are necessary hardships that stretch and grow our faith as we seek to move forward. The right response as we earnestly contend for faith to stand against and overcome these obstacles is to acknowledge our dependence on God.

We do this best by casting our cares on the Lord, trusting that He will somehow work all things together for good.

Know this: God is with us constantly – but especially in the hard times.

Trust in the LORD with all thine heart; and lean not unto thine own understanding .In all thy ways acknowledge him, and he shall direct thy paths (Proverbs 3:3).

"Wesley finds the willpower, determination, and fortitude (known as guts in Arkansas) to do all he can from his wheelchair for the Lord Jesus Christ, whom he deeply loves," shared Rev. Thornton.

"The apostle Paul was arrested and confined, but God used him during that time to write some of the letters in the New Testament. Wesley has now been arrested by ALS and confined to a wheelchair, but God uses him to help others memorize the letters Paul and others wrote in the Bible," added Rev. Thornton.

"In March 2013, I was diagnosed with ALS (Lou Gehrig's disease). I was the under Shepherd for one of God's most loving flocks, New Home Baptist Church, and they did not want me to resign and I did not want to either. So I continued to serve there even confined to a wheel chair until February 2014 when my lung muscles became to weak for me to continue. Now I have no use of my legs, my lung muscles are weak which greatly limits my speaking abilities and my arms and hands are almost useless. I cannot use a standard keyboard or phone. I am typing this with eye recognition technology. Yes sir, I am typing with my eyes."

Wesley's life is built on the simple confession that Jesus is Lord. Jesus is real. Jesus is alive. Jesus is a very present help. Against all (human) odds Wesley has topped that confession with layers of simple everyday accomplishments. These are his daily gifts to God.

"ALS has taken a lot from me but it has not taken my mind or my love for nor my desire to minister to others for my Lord Jesus Christ. I can still talk some but if there is no one in the room with me I cannot answer the phone or call out. Email is the best way for me to communicate or set an appointed time for me to call or be called.

ALS has provided Wesley with a platform, an unusual opportunity to be a witness to Christ. When we give God His rightful place as Lord, His presence strengthen us. God provides help to the helpless, strength to the strengthless and hope to the hopeless. When we are, like Wesley, grounded and rooted in faith God enables us to hold tight to the plow and meet the future with confidence.

ALS And Me
J. Wesley Harville

What do you know about this disease? amyotrophic lateral sclerosis (ALS, or Lou Gehrig's disease).

Four years ago I had only heard of it and really knew nothing about it. Millions of dollars have been raised for research and to assist those living with it and I want to say thank you to all those that have given. Since Lou Gehrig was diagnosed (over 75 years ago) very little has been learned about the cause and there is still no cure.

I would like to share my experience with you. In the summer of 2011 my crew of football officials and I were getting ready for another football season. Studying the rules and running to get in shape. We had a full schedule of regular season games along with several pre-season scrimmages and playoff games ahead of us. But, from the start, I was having trouble breathing and great difficulty running. I finished the most difficult football season of my career. On Sundays I was also having trouble with my voice. No more singing specials and even had to stop singing with the congregation to save my air to preach. It became very hard for me to get up the steps to the pulpit. I was soon using a cane to walk and falls were becoming more frequent. I had always had good health and in my mind I still did. I just did not believe this could be anything serious.

My doctor urged me to have a sleep study. After two sleep studies I was diagnosed with severe sleep apnea. The treatment was to sleep with a Bi-PAP machine. I felt much better and thought I was on my way back. In a few weeks that proved not to be the case. My wife and I were convinced then that the problem had to be my heart but after visit with my cardiologist and a barrage of test my heart was shown to be fine. A healthy heart is good news but walking with the aid of a cane and struggling to breath showed that I had a problem.

After checking myself into the hospital and two weeks of testing and rehab we were told that I had ALS, a disease for which there is no known cure or treatment. That was March 2013.

Today I am in a wheel chair with no use of my legs at all. I still wear my breathing machine (Bi-PAP) twenty-four hours a day seven days a week. Now I am quickly losing the use of my hands. And I am typing this using my eyes.

ALS is a neuro-degenerative disease which randomly turns off motor neurons, causing paralysis of the effected muscle, organ, or limb, but leaving the mind fully intact. Ultimately, most ALS patients end up totally paralyzed before it takes their lives.

Thanks to all that give to the ALS Association and all who have helped to bring awareness to this disease. And a special thank you to all of those who pray for me. My God is good and all knowing and all powerful and ever present and He loves me and you.

"Unanticipated, unexpected burdens often give birth to unanticipated, unexpected blessings. In a circumstance that would cause many to give up, throw in the towel and succumb, Wesley has persevered and written a book, 'Meditate Therein Day And Night' to honor Christ and to bless the people of God's Kingdom. *Published By Parables* is pleased and proud to publish Wesley's gift to God and the people of His Kingdom.

       Dr. John Dee Jeffries
       CEO/Acquisitions Editor
       Published By Parables

Meditate Therein Day And Night
A Scripture Memorization Plan
J. Wesley Harville

Memorize Scripture! That thought causes anxiety and fear for many. But this book, written by J. Wesley Harville, chases the fear and anxiety away.

"The value of God's Word can never be overemphasized," writes Harville, "and learning it should never be diminished."

Use Harville's book to hide God's Word in your heart. Take advantage of the Wesley's labor to help others labor successfully for the Lord.

There is no substitute for meditating and memorizing God's Word and there is no shortcut to having it dwell in us. Harville has developed a passion-filled plan that is purposeful and practical.

Support and encourage Wesley's Ministries
Order your copy today
Available through Amazon,
Barnes and Noble, Books-A-Million,
and wherever fine Christian books are sold.

**Shortly before this book was published
J. Wesley Harville went home to be with the Lord
Two days before he died he was actively
ministering God's Wotd through face book.**

Kathryn Smith
God is Faithful, No Matter What

"Our family was about to face our deepest fear and our greatest challenge. We would have to believe when faith was all we had."

"The doctor said she had less than an hour to live...."

--- Commentary / John Dee Jeffries ---

<u>First Thought</u>: I don't know how convictions are formed, or why they are present in some and absent in others. Someone once likened the building of a conviction to growing a tree, requiring the right seed, time, and care. Perhaps so. I do not know. But I do know this. When convictions are properly formed, Oh! How they grip and how they guide.

<u>Second Thought</u>: I won't presume to know how you know or how you feel when you sense that you're in the presence of the Lord, or that the Lord is speaking to you,

or how it is that you know it is God you are hearing. But, deep down, deep down within, Christian evangelist and author Kathryn Smith knew that she was encountering the Lord and He was speaking…It was the Lord, and she knew that it was the Lord. She was hearing God's calm, quieting, whispering-kind of voice in the midst of the greatest life-or-death crisis she had ever encountered.

"God spoke to me" is one of the most controversial, confusing statements, both inside and outside of the family of God. For some it breeds confusion; for others, misunderstanding. Saying you heard God speak will cause some to question your sanity.

The doctors, nurses, specialists and other authorities disregarded, discountered and doubted Kathy's convictions. They continued to preach their hopeless message of gloom and doom, disability and death – but Kathy would have none of it – She had heard from God.

<u>Final Thoughts</u>: God speaks to people who are ready and prepared to hear Him. You can get into a good place to hear from God by spending daily time reading the Bible and praying. What we learn in <u>private</u> through our Bible readings and prayer become part of what is seen in <u>public</u>. God can speak to anyone, at any time at any place – but He will seldom speak to a person who is not ready to hear.

The Bible is God's Word. It gives us God's guidance for life's problems. God's Word give us the ability to believe when faith is all we have.

My sheep hear my voice, and I know them, and they follow me (John 10:27)

God is Faithful, No Matter What
Kathryn Smith

Our family was about to face our deepest fear and our greatest challenge. We would have to believe when faith was all we had.

On September 22, 1988, my youngest daughter, Amy, was twelve years old, and I was driving her to school. It was just another day. We were talking about moving to a new house and she was laughing. We were only about two miles from home. She rode in the front seat next to me. She wanted a tissue, and the box had slid under the seat. She could not reach it, so she unhooked her seatbelt, just for a second and bent over. In that brief moment, everything changed. Several cars ahead someone looked away from the road to adjust their radio. They ran into the car in front of them. They were hit by the truck behind them. Then the driver in the car behind the truck crashed into it. The driver of the shiny new firebird in front of me never even had time to step on the brake. I did not have time to stop either. My foot pushed the brake to the floor but it was too late. I remember screaming the name of Jesus. When the sound of crunching metal stopped, all I could hear was the constant dinging of an alarm going off. I turned and looked into the passenger seat. There was my precious daughter, her body contorted in a seizure. Her hands were twisted into knots and her eyes were rolled back in her head. She was unconscious. I remember getting out of the car and going around to her side, I wanted to immobilize her neck, in case she had broken it. On the way around the car, I yelled for someone to call 911. Then with no one on earth listening I said firmly, "Devil you cannot have my daughter." I knew I had to take a stand right then if she was going to have any chance to live. I also talked with my Lord while I knelt there holding her head between my hands. I remember speaking directly to Jesus, "Lord if you want her, I will give her to you. If there is any way you can give her back to me, I want her to live, but don't leave her like this. Make her whole or take her with you." I meant all of those words. Deep in my heart I knew it was going to be a hard climb.

When the first fireman arrived he took my place and started an IV there was very little blood in the car. It came from a cut on the back of her head. Amy's face looked perfect; on the outside she was mostly undamaged. She had a second seizure, and I suspected a brain injury. The EMT did this every day, but that was my baby and all of this was torturous to me. The ambulance arrived shortly after they had placed a neck brace on her and started moving her to a backboard. The EMT seemed in a big hurry and asked which hospital. I asked him which was best and he said, "Right now all that matters is which is closest." So we went to St. Anthony's Hospital. I prayed under my breath the whole way there.

When we arrived they did an exam on me while they did CT scans and such on Amy. When they passed me in the hall, I could see her thrashing around on the gurney, and a nurse forcing air into her lungs with a manual ventilator. They said the best Neurosurgeon in town 'just happened' to be in the hospital. The doctor said she had two cerebral hemorrhages, and she had less than an hour to live without surgery. So my husband and I signed consent forms and they rushed her into an operating room. It was five hours later when we got the first report, and another two before the surgery was completed. The surgeon took us into a conference room and told us her chances were not good. If she made it through the day, we would see if she ever woke up. If she did wake up, his belief was that she would basically be a vegetable.

"If she wakes we will find out if she can see, or think, or hear or move." His words tore at my heart and challenged my faith. He said they had drilled three holes in her skull and then cut out a circle of bone about the size of an orange to reduce the pressure from the hemorrhage on the side of her brain. The second cerebral hemorrhage was on the back of her head and it was inoperable. If the swelling in her brain subsided, she could come out of the coma in about three days. It was too dangerous to try to airlift her to a children's hospital. So there lay my little girl, the youngest person who had ever been in the ICU at St. Anthony's Hospital. They tried to tell us what to expect, there would be wires and several monitors and a ventilator to breath for her. She had a probe sticking out of her head, reading brain pressure. They had to shave off most of her hair, but they kept it in a bag to send to the funeral parlor later. [Who says that to a parent?] She had a feeding tube in her nose, three IV's and a catheter. They told us she would be very pale and still unconscious, but we could go see her briefly. None of those words even began to tell how bad it looked when we walked into that room. She looked so small and frail, but at least her face was not contorted and her hands were not knotted into claws. They let my husband and I stay for less than five minutes. They said that even the sound of our footsteps could make her brain swell and that the pressure was her greatest danger. The next twenty-four hours were critical. Everyone I knew was praying. There were at least twenty people from the church with my family in the ICU waiting room most of the time.

Three hours later, Amy sat up in bed and tried to pull out the tube in her nose and the one down her throat. She tried with her right hand first and when she could not reach it because her hands were tied to the bedrails, she tried with her left. To me that showed reasoning, and she was semi-conscious; they immediately sedated her. There was some hope, but the nurses said not to get too excited just yet. They explained that brain injury patients had involuntary movements that did not mean anything and that was part of the reason she was restrained. Amy drifted in and out of a medically induced coma. It was agonizing to see her and it was worse to be forced from her bedside. I had meant the words I spoke to God and I was standing precariously close to the brink. I knew I could lose her if I wavered so I held to the belief that God, who loved her even more than I did was with her.

Amy's brain pressure went up and down. When the pressure was low, we were allowed ten minutes an hour in her room. When it was high we could watch her from behind a window. It was in one of those low pressure times, in the wee hours of the morning that I stood at the foot of her bed singing softly. *Praise the name of Jesus, praise the name of Jesus, He's my rock, He's my fortress, He is my deliverer. In Him will I trust, praise the name of Jesus ...*

I did not know the spiritual value of that praise. I wanted Amy surrounded by the Word, and faith, not listening to the doom the doctors and nurses spoke over her. Eventually they let me put a tape player in her room with praise music day and night but that night it was just my feeble voice and my confidence in the Lord I had trusted with her life.

We camped out in that ICU waiting room twenty-four hours a day. I did my praying in the waiting room bathroom. I would go in all alone and whisper to the only One who could do anything to save her. It was there in that bathroom floor that God gave me a scripture to hang on to.

Isaiah 50:4 (KJV) 4 *The Lord GOD hath given me the tongue of the learned, that I should know how to speak a word in season to him that is weary: he wakeneth morning by morning, he wakeneth mine ear to hear as the learned.*

I took that to mean Amy would wake up and that she would have a normal mind and she would both hear and speak. I clung to that word from God. It was my anchor, driven deep into the bedrock of scripture as Amy and I hung on a lifeline over the gaping abyss of potential death and a mountain of negative reports.

On the third day, she was more active. I told the nurse, "I am a sign language interpreter, and Amy knows a little sign. If she wakes up and can't talk because of all those tubes, she will try to sign. When she does, I will be in the waiting room, call me." She smiled and acted like I was crazy. Later that day, that same nurse summoned me. Amy was moving her hand and when the nurse asked if she was signing and wanted her mom, Amy nodded. I walked into the room, her eyes were still a little hazy but I talked to her and she started spelling out these words, "Am I going to die?" I knew that my answer was vital to her recovery; that question was the one everyone wanted answered. I had one moment to stand strong; I answered with faith. I said "No, Amy you won't die." Then she spelled, "Can

I have a drink of water?" When the nurse said no, Amy started to cry and they sedated her again. That nurse who had so doubted went out in the hall and jumped up and down with me. In the morning when the surgeon made his rounds, he asked me to explain exactly what had happened. I told him that Amy rarely signed, and she had spelled out letter by letter the two complete sentences. He said that was good because at least she could talk with her mother, because she was very unlikely to be able to speak. The injury had been near the speech center of the brain. Again, he gave me a negative report, and again I held to that word in Isaiah.

She was in the ICU for nine days. When she was breathing on her own and the respirator tubes came out she was able to speak in a whisper. I thanked God, but the battle was not over. They moved her to a regular room for another five days. God had been faithful. There were still a few obstacles, and the doctors were not sure what she would be able to do; they were hoping she would walk. We now had assurance that she could hear and speak, but she sounded and acted almost like a two year old. Some of her memories were scrambled. For example, she could not remember her sister's name. She would ask, "Is "sixteen," here?" I would act like that was normal and tell her, "Yes Marie is in the waiting room." Each day I held to those promises in Isaiah 50 and each day there was some improvement. Near the end of our hospital stay, they started her on physical therapy and she started to stand; her balance was off for a short time, but she could walk. She had quadruple vision, but she could see. When her vision corrected itself enough she could read words like "encyclopedia" but not small words like "the, and, or it." Those site words had to be relearned, so did her multiplication tables. When we went for her post-surgery checkup, the surgeon said the second blood clot had mysteriously dissolved. I knew the Lord had removed it. God did what no doctor could. The doctor had a copy of the newspaper with a picture of the accident in her file. She made the front page, but the good news was never printed there. The Surgeon said, "You must have a purpose to be here; you should not have lived. Make something good out of your life." Her doctor wanted her on anti-seizure medicine but she asked me, "Mom did God heal me or not?" When I said yes, she refused to take it. She never did have a seizure.

Today, Amy is forty. She is the mother of four amazing children. She has two degrees and she works as an occupational therapist assistant. She is perfect and whole. She has a scar shaped like a "question mark" on one side of her head and a bald circle the size of a quarter on the back of her head. Fortunately, she has lots of hair to cover them. If you feel her skull there are dents about like the finger holes in a bowling ball. The drill holes never fill in, but the circle of bone was reinserted and grew back fine. Amy is my miracle child. She taught me to trust God when there was no one else to trust. Psalm 50:15 (KJV) *15 And call upon me in the day of trouble: I will deliver thee, and thou shalt glorify me.* God was and is faithful— to Him be all the glory.

He was a stronghold, a fortress when I had my deepest need. Psalm 86:5-7 (KJV) *5 For thou, Lord, art good, and ready to forgive; and plenteous in mercy unto all them that call upon thee. 6 Give ear, O LORD, unto my prayer; and attend to the voice of my supplications. 7 In the day of my trouble I will call upon thee: for thou wilt answer me.* In my day of trouble, I asked for a miracle and I got it. God proved Himself faithful to me, when all the odds were against me.

When you stand in need, trust in Him. God is faithful. If Amy had died, God would not have failed and I would never have turned away from Him. I had committed my heart to follow Him, no matter what. Most of us face at least one moment when we have to put it all on the line. I was willing to stand in that day of trouble. I was so blessed to get what I asked for, she is whole. But God is always our strength and if I had needed Him to stand beside me while I watched her die, I would have found Him faithful there as well. You can trust God; He is faithful, no matter what.

Rev. Kathryn Smith

Kathy Smith was saved in 1972, in a revival at Suburban Baptist Church in Granite City IL. In 1980, after a powerful encounter with the Holy Spirit, at Full Gospel Evangelistic Center of Alton, she began to minister the Word in Power.

"God called me to 'build up the body of Christ,' and I have been preaching and teaching all these years for that purpose."

Becoming an author was a natural expansion of Kathy's call to minister.

She presently serves as an Associate Minister at The House of Victory in Cottage Hills IL, under Pastor Timothy Naylor. She is available for speaking engagements and would gladly come minister at your church or conference.

Contact information
Fire in the Blood Ministries
Rev. Kathy Smith
Email: klssaved1972@yahoo.com
Fire in the Blood Ministries also has a Facebook Page
fbm/revkathy   or   m.me/revkathy

At this writing Kathy has authored three books:
There is Fire in the Blood
Meet Me on the Mountain
I Hear the Rocks Falling
Wilt Thou Be Made Whole

Support and encourage Kathy's Ministries
Order your copies of Kathy's books today
All are available through Amazon,
Barnes and Noble, Books-A-Million,
and wherever fine Christian books are sold.

John Dee Jeffries
Wounded Women – Sad Sex

Her eyes! Her eyes revealed an anguish, an inner anguish that she could not hide. Though it beat in her chest, her heart was a dead heart!

Yes, her heart was dead -- Dead to life. Dead to love. Dead to God. Tortured by her past! Tortured by her secrets! Tortured! Tortured!

Her wounds, her scar tissue – was real, terribly real – and she desperately needed healing!

--- Commentary / John Dee Jeffries ---

Her name was, well, that really doesn't matter. She could be your wife, or your sister, or the gal in the next office – she could be you! (And, I might add, this is not a "female only" issue, but for this venue I'll address it as such.)

She was basically a young believer, in her late forties and saved for less than two years. She was one of the sweetest, happiest people I'd ever met. She loved God, loved God's church and loved her pastor. She had the ability to wiggle her way into your heart, and she did that often, and with many people, both inside and outside the church! Her joy and happiness were contagious, conspicuous and continuous. Everybody was happy when she was around. She carried sunshine wherever she went, wherever she was.

Then one day.....

Yep! There's always that one day, isn't there?

Then one day..... she came into my office wearing a really sad sack kind of face. Nothing fake about what I was seeing either – she was too distant and too distracted and too disturbed in appearance to hide this dour, sour kind of mood.

"What's up with you," says I.

"Nothing."

But, we both knew better. "Sit down, take a load off your mind," says I. "I've never seen you this way -- so depressed, so down! So tell me, what's up? Empty your bucket, tell me about it!"

"Well," says she, after a long pause. "I've been reading this book and it says if 'this something' happened to you when you were a child, then these other things are what will be happening to you when you're an adult!"

What followed was the painful story of a wounded woman, a story I've heard often, more often than any could imagine. Sitting in the shadows of our congregations, and, yes, sometimes standing at the forefront, are wounded women who bear a silent secret of the 'this something' that happened to them– sexual abuse.

After she talked for awhile I assured her that God's Truth could and would "set her free!" – and it did – three days later!

"So you've been reading this book for four days now," says I, "and you find that what the book is saying is true in your life – you're experiencing these things, negative depressive things, and you're depressed, really depressed about that – down in the dumps!"

"Yes," says she. "Yes, I am very much depressed about what I have been reading concerning what is happening with me now and about what will be happening to me in the future."

"Were you depressed last week before you read the book?"

"No," says she, but I didn't KNOW about these things before I read the book."

"No," says I, "let's correct that -- you didn't BELIEVE these things until you read the book! There's a difference!"

She tilted her head and raised one brow, not knowing what to say or what to think.

"Well," says she as the other brow raised, "what do you mean?"

"What I mean is this: before you read this book you were one of the sweetest, happiest people I'd ever met. You were like that because you were reading and believing what God's Word says about you now and what is in store for you in the future. God says, 'You are a new creation now; old things have passed away and all things – everything about you – is new and fresh!' -- right now -- and knowing and believing that made you happy and joyful."

She tilted her head again and raised one brow a second time.

"God says that when you received Christ you were 'born again' and you were born again -- and you experienced a newness of life – and that newness of life, the life of the Spirit of Christ, that made you happy and joyful! You believed what you read about yourself in God's Word and that made you happy and joyful – and you actually became, through the power of God, His Spirit and His Word, a new person altogether – happy, joyful."

She tilted her head yet again then inched closer as I continued to speak.

"Now, for the last four days, you've been reading and believing this other book, a book that describes your old life and the end product of that old life, negative depressive things, and you're depressed, really depressed about that.

That book has become, through your faith in what you have been reading in that book, it has become a self-fulfilling prophecy.

"What that book is talking about, the repercussions of sexual abuse; those consequences are real, very real. That book is talking about the natural consequences of sexual abuse. These things do recur later in life in many who have suffered sexual abuse and they do bind many, many women to the anxious memories of a painful past. They're shackled to that past, in bondage, lacking the emotional strength to set themselves free.

"God's book talks about something that is real too, something more real than any could imagine, something that sets a woman free. God's book speaks about the supernatural consequence of God working in you. He works within you to set you free from the natural consequences of that painful past and from the painful memories of that past too."

The corners of both eyes began to moisten. She reached into her pocket, retrieved a tissue, then wiped the tears away.

"Choose now, but choose carefully, and choose wisely. Which book do you believe, I mean, really believe? Who do you believe -- God or the person who wrote this book? What do you believe has the greater power to set you free? What do you really believe about yourself and about the power of God and His ability to set you free from your past? God says you've been severed from the power of the past and the power of that old life, and a new power, the very power of God has been unleashed and now flows within you and through you. You've been set free!"

Her prescription, with respect to her past and her past experience was as follows: "Go home and give yourself a pity party for three days. On the third day, the day of resurrection, believe, know and trust 'the power of His resurrection' and thank God for that power. You have been – not will be – but have already been set free!"

Final note: God seldom removes painful memories, but He can and does heal them as we bring them to Him! God can and does heal!

--- Commentary / Additional Notes ---

"Turn your wounds into wisdom," said an anonymous poet! "Most things break, including hearts," added another.

In "Harry Potter and the Order of the Phoenix" J. K Rowling writes – "Some wounds run too deep for healing."

On the opposite end of the spectrum is the old adage "Time heals all wounds!"

Just about everyone has an opinion, a thought, an idea – about woundedness, brokenness – and healing. And therein lies the fly in the ointment! Some falsely believe that "some wounds run too deep" – and cannot be healed! While others mistakenly put faith in the passage of time to heal!

Know this! Time heals nothing! Only Christ, only Christ, truly heals! Know this! There is no wound so deep, so hidden, that Christ cannot reach it – and heal it!

Roughly two years later the lady described in this mini-message died an untimely death. It was a traffic accident followed by a massive heart attack. After the funeral her sister approached me about making an appointment for a counseling session.

Later in the week as we sat and talked I couldn't help but notice her eyes, so much like her now deceased sister; with one major difference.

Her eyes revealed an anguish, an inner anguish that she could not hide. It was an inner anguish that her now deceased sister did not have. Though this anguish beat in her chest, her heart was a dead heart! Yes, her heart was dead -- Dead to life. Dead to love. Dead to God. Tortured by *her* past! Tortured by *her* secrets! Tortured! Tortured! Tortured! Her wounds, her scar tissue – was real, terribly real – and she desperately needed what her deceased sister found through faith in Christ -- she needed healing!

No matter who you are. No matter where you are. There is help -- and hope -- for you! Know this – God loves you and has a wonderful plan for your life. He can and He will heal your wounds.

Know this – there is a part that is God's that you cannot do. (He will do His part, count on it). And, there is a part that is yours that God will not do.

Listen carefully – not too, too far from where you are God has strategically placed a church, a warm, loving, nurturing, deeply spiritual church family who will love you and surround you with God's love.

And, there, leading that church, is a wise pastor that God has placed there – just for you! Draw on his wisdom, his strength and his awareness of God's healing – that pastor is there – he's God's man -- waiting just for you!

Published By Parables
Dr. John Dee Jeffries
CEO-Acquisitions Editor
www.PublishedByParables.com

Pastor
First Baptist Church Chalmette, LA 70043
Email: FBC.Chalmette@gmail.com

At this writing John has authored six books:
The Last Martyr
When I Can't Find God
Hip. Hip. Hallelujah! (A 3-Volume Collection) and
Broken Beyond Belief -- But Not Beyond Faith

Order copies of John's books today
All are available through Amazon,
Barnes and Noble, Books-A-Million,
and wherever fine Christian books are sold.

BROKEN BEYOND BELIEF -- BUT NOT BEYOND FAITH

Martina Gallegos
The Night My Life Began

I was watching a wedding on TV with some of my siblings, and my daughter, at fourteen, was in her bedroom. I needed my glasses, so I tried to reach for them but noticed things were looking very blurry; I tried to blink to see if I'd pass but didn't. I then noticed something weird on the left side of my face; it was numb, so I slapped it a couple of times then proceeded to feel the left side of my body; it, too was numb. I immediately told my family, "Call 911! Something is very wrong.

--- Commentary / John Dee Jeffries ---

We like stories that have Happy Endings, dislike stories with Unhappy Endings and distain stories that are filled with injustice, wrongdoing and other bad stuff. Whether the story is in a book, a movie, a song or real life, we all understand that life and its stories don't always have happy endings. As shared in the prologue, bad stuff happens to bad people, to good people, to God's people, to all people. Such is life in a fallen universe.

Simply stated, we live in an environment where bad stuff happens. Bad stuff is all around us – it happens. So, we trudge on, day after day, doing our best to create our happily-ever-after when suddenly….one day…

One Day….. yes, there's always that One Day…

Then One Day, the sad story knocks at the door of our life – and bad stuff happens -- to us or someone we love. The unthinkable happens. Suddenly something unimaginable occurs. In a singular moment injustice, pain and suffering raps on the door of your house -- What happens then?

You'll stand there, stunned…facing sorrow full face; you're broken beyond belief. What happens then? You stand there…shocked…looking evil straight in the eye! You pray that things will work out; but they don't. Nothing is working out the way you had hoped. Things get worst, terribly worst -- not better. What happens then?

When it becomes obvious that we're not going to live happily-ever-after – there are some things we should know:

(1) The Story is not over!

(2) If you're a believer in Christ, life in this fallen universe is the worse it will ever be! If you're not a believer in Christ, life in this fallen universe is the best it will ever get!

(3) No matter what has come or does come into your life or marred your life – Romans 8:28 will win out in the end and – through the power of Christ you will live happily-ever-after! And, that puts a smile on the face, hope in the heart, and courage in the spirit!

But, wait, let's ask one important question: What happens if the one day that ushers in darkness is the day you were born – and every day that flows from that one day drags on and on and on; filled with sorrow?

The Night My Life Began
Martina Gallegos

Picture it. The year? 1964. A child is born – a baby girl. Martina Gallegos The place? Potrero de Gallegos, Zacatecas, Mexico. A large family -- five brothers and three sisters – celebrated baby Martina's birth. The place was hot. Mexico hot. One word, one singular word, described the plight of Martina's family: Poverty – not just ordinary poverty, but severe poverty. In her early childhood years Martina knew nothing but poverty and all of the bad stuff that came with being poor.

"I was born into severe poverty. My father worked hard, extremely hard, in the fields, struggling to harvest whatever the land would yield. Sometimes, no, change that, many times, I remember, many times we had nothing to eat.

"My dad always did the very best that he could to feed our large family but sometimes things didn't work out.

We'd run out of beans and corn, our staple food. When that happened my dad would bring veggies, fruit, or different kinds of berries and cacti from the fields. We would eat that until we could get more beans and corn."

Today, through sociological and psychological studies, we have a better understanding of the effects of the constant worry and stress associated with severe poverty -- on parents, their marriages, their families and their extended families. Sociologists, psychologists, the medical community understand many of the physical and emotional problems associated with poverty: stress, depression, post traumatic stress disorder and the debilitating affects on children, parents and the extended family.

"A few times my dad got so sick we thought we'd lose him. Somehow, I don't know how, my dad always seemed to recover. Because of the hard work my dad did in the fields and because of his bouts with sickness, the stress impacted the whole family, not just the children, but our extended family too.

"My mom was practically raising all of us kids by herself. That caused added stress. I began to see a distance between my parents when I was still too young to understand what was going on. They hardly spoke to each other and didn't look at one another when they did. They started sleeping in separate beds and rooms. I was about nine or ten. I was older enough to know that something was not right. I could feel it."

When there is relational stress between parents, the children, feeling that stress, will often step in between the parents in an effort to divert the stress, stop the argument or avoid physical altercations.

"I took care of dad when he came home from the fields.

He would bring firewood home to keep us warm during the winter and he would keep some firewood to sell."

The stress, the anxiety and feelings of nervousness increased within the family through the nearly constant bickering with Martina's grandmother and her aunts. Martina's dad could never please them. They constantly put Martina's father down for being lazy. The grandmother's sarcasm; the cutting remarks by the aunts, their snide, harsh words, and their scornful sneers…it was maddening.

"I hated that. I hated that kind of thinking," said Martina. "It always bothered me, always."

Life and its bad stuff was happening, spinning out of control. Things started to get out of hand.

"My father started beating my mother almost everyday. I don't know how long my dad did that. I just know that my dad kept beating my mom. The beatings finally stopped when my older brother grew tall enough and strong enough to stand up to our dad…then the beatings stopped."

Life and its bad stuff, however, did not stop. It continued to spin out of control.

"My mom suffered a huge abdominal hernia doing chores for her mom. I always thought that was strange, my mom doing chores for her mom. My grandmother despised not only my dad, but my mom too, ever since childhood."

Time passed. The bad stuff within the family continued spinning out of control. Martina, who was growing older and taller, entered a stage of rebellion. She refused to wash dishes, refused to help wash the family pets (including some birds that her mother deeply loved). Martina refused to do her chores.

Life and its bad stuff was still spinning out of control.

"My mom suffered a stroke. She was only 35 yrs old. I didn't know. I really didn't know what had happened. One minute mom was okay; the next, well, mom could barely walk or speak, and her left side was pretty much limp. I felt sad and worried about mom and about our family. I don't recall my age but I was younger than twelve.

"God? Don't ask me about God. I was too angry at the world to think about God."

Miraculously, Martina's mother eventually recovered completely, or so it appeared. Later, Martina and her mother emigrated to the United States. ("Mom chose me to come along," said Martina). Martina's father chose to stay in Mexico.

"My mother became mentally ill shortly after we emigrated to the United States. Unfortunately, I lost my mother to suicide. My entire world came tumbling down.

"For the first time in my life I actually passed out, landing hard on the floor. My mom was about 44 years old when she committed suicide. I was 16 years old.

"I don't think God was in the picture at that point. Uncles and aunts took my younger siblings, and I stayed with my recently married older brother. That was an unfortunate decision that I made. (That's another story).

Nevertheless, time passed. Two years later, still bearing the wounds of her mother's suicide, Martina finished high school. She then enrolled in college. Things seemed to finally be headed in the right direction. Life and its bad stuff, however, were still spinning out of control.

"I was in college when it happened. I lost one of my sisters to suicide. I couldn't believe it. I felt completely numb. I couldn't believe 'God' would put me through this again."

The shock and grief of suicide is complicated. Your thoughts continuously twist and turn back on themselves, like a maze constantly turning in on itself. You're confronted by one question, then wrestle with the next, then mysteriously find yourself back at the first question, yet again. It's a constant barrage of questions that have no answer -- "what if" and "should have" and "why didn't I." And the anger. Martina wanted to scream, wanted to punch a wall. She wanted to shake her sister, then felt the pain of wanting to hug her -- and knowing that they would never hug again.

If the burden of losing her sister, accompanied with the dredging up of the previous loss of her mother by suicide weren't enough, Martina began having trouble at school.

"I began having trouble with bullying at school. I was distraught at being away from my home, a home I never really had. I was dealing with depression. I lost my mom and now my sister to suicide. I began to worry about my own mental health. I sought psychological help on campus to deal with my loss, my health issues, and my life....I thought I'd drop out of school but eventually chose instead to stay and work my heart out."

No one knows the source of that keep-on-keeping-on mentality – but Martina had it. Was it rooted and developed as a survival mechanism through her dysfunctional family of origin? Martina certainly learned how to survive there. Did the challenges brought into her early life by the grandmother and aunts create the drive to preserve? Or did the migration to the U.S. enable Martina to develop the tenacity and inner strength to move forward in life, even though bad things kept on happening?

What about God? If God had a role in shaping this

element of Martina's character, His presence wasn't conspicuous and His work wasn't obvious. If anything it seems that God was held at bay by Martina's anger.

"I graduated with my B. A. then I earned teaching credential and quickly landed a teaching job. I was excited about this opportunity then….discrimination. I was discriminated against, repeatedly. I was 'The Mexican Teacher,' the know-nothing, the nobody with no rights of any kind, the punching-bag, and I taught in the classroom for 'reject students.'

"I can't believe in a God who's supposed to see and make everything happen."

The tendency to see meaning in the events and experiences of life is rooted in Christian and religious belief. Seeking meaning, however, is also a part of human nature. People in general, even the irreligious, seem to posses a powerful drive to make sense out of life. This drive usually kicks in when bad things happen. When meaning is not found it is not uncommon for antagonism to strike out against God.

"Again, I thought I'd quit but didn't."

Three years later Martina was viciously assaulted by a student in a classroom. Even though the student had a history of violence and was known by the school district for his violence, the forces of discrimination were slanted against Martina. An administratively negligent school system, institutional fear, psychological biased evaluations and other factors worked against Martina.

"I was always in fear of another attack after that."

Someone suggested that Martina quit, or transfer to another school.

"I told them I wasn't the problem; I was a good teacher.

Parents appreciated my support and felt comfortable with me. I spoke their language and their children actually learned in my class."

Martina stayed with the school system and maintained a good rapport with and advocated for students and parents.

"I remained at the same district, site, and grade levels for eighteen years till I suffered a work injury."

Then, a major decision.

"I got married. Then, a few years later, I had my daughter…

"Then, I couldn't believe it. I was 32 years old, only 32 years old, when the unthinkable happened – I ended up in a Women's Shelter. While living at the Women's Shelter, I commuted to work every morning. I would drop my daughter off at a sitter and pick her up after work before driving 45 minutes back to the shelter."

After years of enduring life and all of the bad stuff that came against her, after years of negative, mean-spirited people trying to bully her, and after the loss of her mom and sister to suicide, one can easily see that Martina had built up quite a store of depression, anger, resentment, bitterness and more.

In 2 Corinthians 4 the apostle Paul, who had his share of tough times, writes that even the bad stuff of life "works for us."

He offers the following encouragement, "So we're not giving up. How could we! Even though on the outside it often looks like things are falling apart on us…These hard times are small potatoes… (The Message).

A stonemason strikes a rock ninety-nine times with no success, not even a crack on the surface on the rock. Then, with blow one hundred, the rock splits in two. It was not the last blow that split the rock, but all the blows that had gone before.

Martina titled her manuscript for this project "The Night My Life Began" – and described that night with these words…

"….When I look back at the night of July 8th, 2012, I still can't believe how close I was to death, and how staying alive has become a constant, challenging, and rewarding battle these many years later.

"I'd been having pain on the back of my neck for a couple of weeks, but neither my PCP nor I made much of it because I'd had regular check-ups, and nothing seemed to be wrong. He did suggest, strongly, that I watch my diet because I was showing signs of being pre-diabetic and my blood pressure was a bit elevated; had I been then who I am today, I'd have told him I was in trouble, and the fact that my work environment, neighborhood, and family had been a mess for years didn't help either. The world had turned a deaf ear on me, so I kept things to myself.

"I was watching a wedding on TV with some of my siblings, and my daughter, at fourteen, was in her bedroom. I needed my glasses, so I tried to reach for them but noticed things were looking very blurry; I tried to blink to see if I'd pass but didn't. I then noticed something weird on the left side of my face; it was numb, so I slapped it a couple of times then proceeded to feel the left side of my body; it, too was numb. I immediately told my family, "Call 911! Something is very wrong. I knew I wasn't having a heart attack, so I was sure it was a stroke. For a second I figured it was my time to go, and I felt deep peace, but then I thought about my daughter, and my fighting spirit kicked in. I'd lost my own mother when I was sixteen. I heard commotion up and down the stairs.

"The paramedics asking me for my name, location at that moment, and some other stuff I can't recall, but I recall answering each question; however, one of my brothers says once I said to call 911, I went limp. I even recall when my brother kept telling me to take breaths."

After being transported to St. John's Hospital the seriousness of Martina's condition became apparent.

"My situation was grave. I had suffered a massive hemorrhagic stroke, and the hospital didn't have the proper equipment to treat me. I was transported by ambulance to Santa Barbara because the helicopter was not available.

"A Dr. Zauner a neurosurgeon, served as the lead doctor. I was placed on medically induced coma, and doctors performed a craniotomy to suction the blood and release pressure, and I was later told my brain was so swollen it was at risk of exploding. My family was told that the doctors had done all they could and to get ready for the worse, but after twenty-two days in a coma, I woke up.

"I remember when I first came out of the coma how much I loved God. He'd always walked alongside me; when I was a child, I'd always felt His presence. His presence was even stronger after my near, so near fatal stroke. I loved Him so much, I'd talk with Him daily but especially at night, and I started writing how I felt about Him."

Eventually Martina was transferred to a rehab hospital. She did make one important decision – she would meet the challenges of life head-on instead of head-down.

"I had no idea what kind of world I'd face, but once I got to the rehab hospital, I promised myself I'd do everything morally and legally right to get back on my feet, and I stuck to that promise."

Martina started a regiment of solid physical, occupational, psychological, and speech therapy -- and the therapeutic staff had a motto from the start: No ifs, no butts, and that suit Martina just fine. She did everything asked of her and never complained, no matter how much it hurt.

"I felt like Humpty-Dumpty being put back together again."

A major complication was the ongoing, lingering pain from Achilles surgery that Martina had just two weeks before her stroke.

"You'd think physical therapy would be the most painful, but it was actually speech therapy that caused greater pain. Speech therapy forced me to think, and intentional thinking literally made my brain hurt. I was physically drained half way through the sessions, but I never stopped; even the therapist would suggest I take a break, but I never did."

Martina completed her rehab and returned home.

"I needed people who were supportive, positive, and who knew or cared to ask what was going on with me, or what I was already doing to meet my medical needs.

"I was happy to be home with my daughter and pets, but very soon the walls begin to shrink; I knew I needed to get out of the house… I was getting very depressed and knew how dangerous that was, so I went to a local hospital to see if they needed volunteers.

Martina began volunteer work in the Surgery Waiting room. Even though she volunteered only three hours a day, three days a week, she enjoyed her volunteerism.

"I needed more to keep my brain busy, so I called my local elementary school since I couldn't go to my site due to my work injury. I began working another two days, two hours a week. I was enjoying and feeling productive when one day....

One Day..... yes, there's always that One Day...

One day a psychiatrist put an end to Martina's volunteerism. She became very depressed and suicidal, so...

"...I knew I had to find other things to do; so I continued writing and picked up Italian. I resumed a Master's degree and started publishing. I also enjoyed gardening and going for walks; I'd begun retraining for driving. I knew ground school was no longer possible, so I looked for and found an online program; I was aware I'd face cognitive challenges because my brain was still pretty damaged, but I went for it. Turns out, my brain was the least of my challenges, it was dealing with staff and administrators that almost caused me my degree, but I persevered despite almost quitting a handful of times. I'd never quit before, and I wasn't going to start now.

"Despite all the familiar obstacles and frustrations, I graduated with my Master's the same year two of my poems were published in an anthology, and my daughter graduated from high school.

"The following year I published my first book, a mixture of poetry and prose, all autobiographical. I'd already become an award winning poet before I'd published my first book; I published my second book last year, and I'm currently working on my third, a bilingual one.

"Because I hadn't been doing new things for brain work, I decided to pick up Portuguese, and I still practice

Italian. I learned early after my stroke, that it's essential for recovery to do things I've never done before: learning new languages, music, art, volunteering, exercising, word games, writing, knitting, gardening. ...

"It's imperative for any kind of survivor to remain physically, intellectually, socially, and spiritually engaged in order to gain any degree or complete recovery.

"I wouldn't be completely honest if I said I wasn't in conflict with God. I sometimes feel that I had a love-hate relationship with Him. I couldn't reconcile all the chaos in the world when God just sat down and watched, let it happen; I've had some frustrating, troubling times in my life…but I was determined to keep believing and keep my faith intact. I still love God as much as I did when I was a child and hope things will get better for my daughter, for me, and within me, and the world.

Contact information

At this writing Martina Gallegos has authored two books:

Grab the Bull by the Horns -
Escaped Death to Face Hell
and
Steppingstones -
Journal to Recovery from Stroke and Brain Injury

Order your copies of Martina's books today
All are available through Amazon,
Barnes and Noble, Books-A-Million,
and wherever fine Christian books are sold.

Jane Daly
The Greatest Loss

Like a head-on collision, the world stops in an instant. We're initiated into a club whose membership we never asked for. A hole is created in us that can't be filled.

That is what happened when my son was diagnosed with terminal cancer at the age of twenty-nine.

When your child dies, it's the feeling of being doused with kerosene and set on fire. It's like having your heart removed while it's still beating. It's a sucker punch to the gut, a baseball bat to the head, and the rug pulled out from underneath you. You lie comatose on the floor, wondering if you'll ever be able to breathe again, and wondering if you want to.

--- Commentary / John Dee Jeffries ---

Sometimes, especially during life's darker days, trusting God is difficult. Yet, this much is certain: whatever your circumstances, you can trust God! The secret to moving forward is to nourish your faith as best as you are able. Invest in Bible study, prayer, meditation, and worship.

Sometimes it's hard to trust God! Sometimes, walking by faith is a bummer! But, keep walking…and keep trusting…. God knows where you are and what you're dealing with – at this very moment!

The Greatest Loss
Jane Daly

The death of a child has been called the greatest loss.

Nothing prepares a mother for the passing of a child. A mother carries a baby inside for nine months. He's part of her. He shares her food and air. He feels his mother's emotions, hears her voice. They're connected by something greater than the slim tether of an umbilical cord.

Love at first sight becomes more than a romantic ideal. From the moment a baby is born, he's the sole object of her adoration. He's perfect, beautiful. He'll be the smartest, cutest, best baby ever born.

In this one brief moment, we mirror God, having created a person solely dependent upon us for everything. We get a glimpse and better understanding of God's great and sacrificial love for us as we sacrifice for our child.

We have a firmer grasp of God's providential care as we provide for our children's needs.

As a baby grows, a mother is his world. When he cries, he wants his mother. When he's hungry, he needs his mother. How many times have you seen a child fall and scrape his knee? The first thing he says is, "I want my mommy!"

We foresee a bright, shiny future for our children. We want for them everything that's been denied to us. The opportunities we've let slip by, we grasp onto for our child.

Everything changes when he is snatched away.

Like a head-on collision, the world stops in ***an instant.*** We're initiated into a club whose membership we never asked for. A hole is created in us that can't be filled.

That is what happened when my son was diagnosed with terminal cancer at the age of twenty-nine.

We'd faced cancer together when he was a junior in high school. At seventeen, his priorities were sports, church, and girls. Cancer wasn't in his plan. He was diagnosed with Hodgkins, which of all the cancers, the most treatable. After nine long months of chemotherapy and radiation, he was pronounced in remission.

Fast forward eleven years. Bobby was married, had a successful business, and owned a beautiful home in Colorado. One Sunday evening in January, we received a phone call.

When the phone rang that January evening in 2009, I had no idea my life was about to change forever. Mike picked up the phone, and as usual, put it on speaker. It was Bobby.

"I need to talk to you and Mom," he told his dad.

I dried my hands while walking from the kitchen to the dining room, dread settling in my stomach like a stone. My instincts told me this wouldn't be a "Hey, I have great news!" kind of a call.

Bobby told us he'd been having health problems. Pressure in his chest. The doctors didn't know what was wrong, and a chest x-ray and MRI were inconclusive. He was going in for exploratory surgery in ten days.

What was going on? Surely it couldn't be cancer. He'd been well for eleven years. He was twenty-nine years old, healthy and active. His business was thriving and he and his wife, Ali, had purchased their first home after five years of marriage. This would be a blip, something to fix and move on. Right?

I flew to Colorado to be with him and Ali during the surgery. Bobby picked me up from the airport. On the way to his house, he asked me, "Remember when I had cancer?"

I nodded.

"Remember how I broke my finger, and that's when they found the tumors?"

I nodded again, wondering where this was going.

His eyes met mine across the small interior of the car. "I broke my finger last week."

That's the moment I entered denial.

Denial takes us away from faith, away from God's divine plan. I didn't want to believe that God would allow my golden child to face cancer again.

My prayers were a mixture of disbelief that this was happening, and entreaty to let it be something other than cancer.

I sat in the hospital waiting room with Bobby's wife and her family. When the surgeon appeared eight long hours later, he confirmed my worst fear. "Your son has cancer." Four words I never thought I'd hear again.

Bobby fought like a trouper for the next year. Chemo robbed him of his hair, but not his spirit. I watched my brave son slowly lose the battle of his life. His faith in God encouraged and uplifted me. Many times he said he knew his life was in God's hands.

When your child dies, it's the feeling of being doused with kerosene and set on fire. It's like having your heart removed while it's still beating. It's a sucker punch to the gut, a baseball bat to the head, and the rug pulled out from underneath you. You lie comatose on the floor, wondering if you'll ever be able to breathe again, and wondering if you want to.

During that final year of my son's life, I lived in Psalm twenty-three. Yea, though I walk through the valley of the shadow of death, I will fear no evil: for thou art with me; thy rod and thy staff they comfort me. (Psalms 23:4 KJV)

I was in a dark valley. There was light at the end, but, first, I had to walk through it. The way seemed endless.

"He leads me beside still waters. He restores my soul," (Psalm 23:2-3 NKJV). This is the part of the Psalm I'd been missing. In his book, A Shepherd Looks at Psalm 23, W. Phillip Keller says:

"We live a most uncertain life. Any hour can bring disaster, danger and distress from unknown quarters. Life is full of hazards. No one can tell what a day will produce in new trouble. We live either in a sense of anxiety, fear, and foreboding, or in a sense of quiet rest. Which is it?"

He reminds the reader that we walk through the valley. We don't stop and live there, nor do we die there. Through all the circumstances I face in life, God continually restores my soul, if I allow him full rein.

I thought my life would stop when Bobby breathed his last breath. I held his hand and stroked his head as he passed from this life into the next.

In that moment, I experienced the truth that we will all die sometime, but Jesus has overcome death.

Gerald Sittser, in A Grace Disguised, says it this way:

"My experience has only confirmed in my mind how hard it is to face loss and how long it takes to grow from it. But it has also reminded me how meaningful and wonderful life can be, even and especially in suffering."

Was I broken from my son's death? Yes, but restored to wholeness by the Lord's handiwork.

The Japanese art of kintsugi uses a special lacquer dusted with powdered gold to repair broken pottery. Nothing is ever truly broken - that's the philosophy behind this unique art. This is a beautiful picture of how God repairs our brokenness, and makes us into something more beautiful than we could imagine.

Contact information
At this writing Jane Daly has authored two books:

Because of Grace,
A Mother's Journey From Grief to Hope
and
The Caregiving Season,
Finding Grace to Care for Your Aging Parent

Order your copies of Jane's books today
All are available through Amazon,
Barnes and Noble, Books-A-Million,
and wherever fine Christian books are sold.

Broken Beyond Belief -- But Not Beyond Faith

Lisa Denny
The Making Of A Jewel
The Diaries. A testimony of one rescued from the Pit

My family life I have been told was abusive. My legs showed the strap marks of father's belt. I struggled to feel that I belonged, was good enough. Mother informed me one day that I was conceived so that her and father would be allowed to marry. So I was a bastard. I was about seventeen. My younger brother tried to run me over with the tractor when I was about eighteen because I disagreed with him while feeding sheep.

Dreams can shatter turning everything into a waste land of darkness scattered with the sharp splinters of regrets, 'what if's' and guilt, of scribbled statements like – The only end to this eternal misery I inflict on others and myself is my death. And I would welcome it if not for the fear that it would hurt others.

--- Commentary / John Dee Jeffries ---

The Bible promises this: tough times are temporary but God's love endures forever! So what does this mean to you? Just this: from time to time everybody faces hardships and disappointments – even disappointment with God – and so will you. When tough times arrive, God always stands ready to protect you and help you. Your task is straightforward – you must share your burdens with Him.

Remember this: Keep on believing! You've not lost everything until you've lost your faith! And that's a choice – never an accident!

The Making Of A Jewel
Lisa Denny

'Whatever makes us more and more able to enjoy making much of God is a mercy. For there is no greater joy than joy in the greatness of God. And if we must suffer to see this and savor it most deeply, then suffering is a mercy. And Christ's call to take up our cross and join Him on the Calvary road is love.'[1]

I had to ask. "Excuse me, but could you explain what a lifelong order means please?" "Just that. Life long." "But…" "Lifelong. Unless you come back and apply for it to be changed." "But how will I know if it would be safe to do so?" "That I cannot answer," and her heels rhythmically echoed as she departed through the court doors.

Lifelong? LORD? I had only wanted six months, at the most a year…..Lifelong…..I was numb except for those two words drumming through my body….Why?

It's been four years without an answer. I don't really expect one this side of Heaven. In many ways I don't need one. Since the late 1990's God has been showing me who He really is, teaching me over and over that He is trustworthy. That He is a good, good God. Always. That He alone is enough even when I feel that I'm being ripped apart and find myself wondering how many times a heart can be broken and still survive.

I cannot remember a time when I did not believe that there had to be a God, a creator God, someone bigger that my father or grandfather, someone in charge of everything. I was about seven when I heard a sermon on Hell, a place of fire and brimstone. I did not know what brimstone was but we had lost a lot of the farm and stock with a bush fire recently so I knew what fire was, what it smelt like and I was not going to live there! So I trusted in this Jesus, the Son of God that I cut out of Christmas cards during Sunday school, who shone in rainbow hues from sunlit windows, gently smiling at children and carrying lambs in His arms, who gave us a reason for Christmas pudding and gifts.

As a teenager I wrote in my diary – Last night I signed a statement saying that through God I have eternal life. As long as my faith grows I know I will do well in this land so that I will be ready to go home to the Kingdom of God. I will have His strength to help me over the problems that seem so bad and unpassable. My family life I have been told was abusive. My legs showed the strap marks of father's belt. I struggled to feel that I belonged, was good enough. Mother informed me one day that I was conceived so that her and father would be allowed to marry. So I was a bastard. I was about seventeen. My younger brother tried to run me over with the tractor when I was about eighteen because I disagreed with him while feeding sheep.

Paying my own way, studying and working hard my dream of being a nurse became reality. So did marriage. My first date with Joe occurred four days after this diary entry – Sunset on Sorrento beach. God if it is your will, take my life into your hands – and my life became swallowed up in his. Several years later I was allowed to have children; Tyler, then four years later Alyssa. All I had ever dreamed for….but dreams can shatter turning everything into a waste land of darkness scattered with the sharp splinters of regrets, 'what if's' and guilt, of scribbled statements like – The only end to this eternal misery I inflict on others and myself is my death. And I would welcome it if not for the fear that it would hurt others.

I remember a certain stretch of road one wet dark night when the oncoming semitrailer's lights beckoned. It would have only taken a slight turn of the wheel on that narrow country road….but to take the kids with me, my sleeping trusting joy of my life kids?…did I have that right?... would they really be better off with Joe or dead with me?....what if they survived?....the moment passed as this mental argument took place…

Joe was a misogamist. I became what he said I was – a stupid fat lazy b****, a big disappointment, a waste of space….no one could blame him if he had an affair while I was so fat and repulsive when pregnant….he did, even bringing her to visit while Ty and I were still in the hospital and there were others. My brother and parents saw him with her as they left visiting their first grandchild but never said for over thirteen years as they were afraid he would stop them seeing him.

Tyler was challenging. The speech therapist said he had no short term auditory memory probably as a result of his traumatic birth. Joe frequently voiced his opinion, loudly and uncaring who heard...he would never forgive me for giving him such a son. Sex had become a violent, gymnastic event leaving bruises and a feeling of being filthy. My 'no's' went unheard. So it was a small relief that it occurred only a few times a year.

As I was driving home from a hellish family holiday Joe became so enraged about the route I had chosen that he undid his safety belt, yelling and swearing abuse opening the door to get out despite the car travelling at about 90kms...I saw the fear and confusion on the kids' faces in the revision mirror and I saw, really saw... I felt an incredible calm come over me....I knew that this insane way of living was going to stop now. After he had left for work the next day Tyler eight and Alyssa four, were like little unstoppable whirlwinds going methodically through each room thinking of things I'd not considered packing. He collected his bags after work, thanking me for saving him the trouble rather colourfully. Sagging against the wall after closing the door on my marriage, my life, my heart cried out, 'Get me out of this and I'll come back to church', not really sure if God was able to see, hear or do anything, or even if He was real. The smouldering candle struggling to be alive, that was inside, which was me, roared into glorious warmth, a brilliant steady flame. Everything was abruptly deafeningly still and quiet. Hope and joy swirled around and settled inside me. I became aware I could dream and that I had not for so very long. There was a tomorrow. I, yes, I, could have a tomorrow! 'All the way, no matter what LORD' became my mantra, 'just don't leave me.'

And He hasn't.

Not when facing the lies of Joe's barrister in a Melbourne court.

Not when my brother refused to have anything to do with me as I'd left such a good man and got religious. Not when my family voiced their disproval that I had become too serious about this religious nonsense and it was time to throw the crutch away surely?

Not when I struggled with what I believed, or even if I did, as emotions swang wildly with the turbulences and pain of access and Joe's ever changing demands.

Not when my pastor had to remove Tyler from home, fearful that come morning Ally and I would not be alive. Not when I had to sign papers almost fifteen years after carrying him in my womb, saying that I refused to provide my son with a safe place to live, handing him over to the Warden of the Courts.

Not when I refused to put off my marriage to Luke because of all the stress with Tyler.

Not when I could not defend myself against the accusations of getting rid of Tyler so I could have an easy life with Luke that came from all directions, even from my church family.

Not when Ally started to talk about what really happened to her on access and began to starve herself. Not when intimacy with Luke became scary and unwanted, plagued with flashbacks.

Not when my church family started to rip itself apart and both 'sides' considered me to be in the enemy camp.

Not when Tyler threatened to kill one of his caseworkers and had to be locked up in a secure house in Melbourne to dry out.

But then in the diary over a period of a few months is this – The darkness is closing, suffocating. Hope? I see none. Oh, Lord that You would give me some! There is no light. I don't want to go through this darkness. I'm afraid. You seem distant. The darkness is always inside…it is just there a sad darkness. But it has changed, become different, starting to consume. There is a wall. You are not there. My prayers bounce off the ceiling. Your Words blur, make no sense. Stubbornly I refuse to stop opening my Bible, searching for You, but there seems to be no point. You have gone and I don't understand….where are You?.....

The psalms – You created the darkness You are in it (Ps.139:11,12; 39:7)….

My hope is in You LORD hold me do not let me go. I want to hold on to You but it is so dark in this part of me I cannot see You when I look. There is no light. Just endless darkness – but You created it. You must be there. And if You are it must be okay…..

And so I learnt a never to be forgotten lesson -

Your presence is far, far more needed than anything You could give or do. (Ps. 18. Especially v.11&28)…..

Does not being able to see the blue sky when it is blanketed by a thick smoke haze from the bushfires mean it is not there, that it is not blue?

No.

So when I cannot see You that does not mean You are not there, just the same as always. I can look through the smoke cloud with eyes of faith and see the blue sky because I know it is there. Can I not look through the darkness with eyes of faith and see You because You are there always?…. for if You were not there I would not be here.

And He did not leave when Tyler at eighteen, skilled at messaging on a mobile – 'ya shold not drive wit cut brake line haha' - and licensed to drive started to bring increasing fear into our lives, and that of our neighbours.

Not when Mark, Luke's son rings telling us that Alyssa does not want to return home. She has been cutting herself because of our oppressive excessive religious attitudes. Jo, Mark's wife, said that they both strongly believed it was not over us disciplining her (for disappearing out a window at night while in an interstate holiday park) but over our beliefs and that was why they were giving her a safe place to stay, where she would be listened to and not judged.

(Mark and Jo are not believers, we had thought Ally was.) I was allowed to visit and hear what was required of us for Ally to return home and not climb out her window at night. Cost is great – reads the diary entry – Lord. I was told if I gave You up I'd have Tyler back, well here I go again….

Ally left home the following year, I asked her to leave as her 'trust me's' about behaviour with yet another boyfriend were shown to be lies. She moved in with him that night. She was not yet sixteen.

Not when I started with a Christian counsellor and started medication for Post-Traumatic Stress Disorder. And not when Tyler rammed our unoccupied parked car at night outside the Pastor's home. There had been several close calls on the road over the past year. Tyler was beginning to act out his threats. Still I hesitated to seek the intervention order that the Police highly recommended….. not sure I can bear this, are You sure Lord? Is this what You really want of me Lord, to hand him over, reject him again?....Do I really have to? I'm not sure You and I agree on what I can cope with, the amount of pain I can live with Lord!

Some days later there was a message in a high pitched squeaky sing-song little kid like voice – Lisa's car gonna to get ******up again permanently....its gonna to be a right off if gonna ignore me....(There was more but forgive me I don't want to remember.)

I had my answer.

The Judge gave his – Your – ruling: Lifelong. Forever… that's a really long time Lord!

My last memory of seeing my son is of him roaring past our home in his car, finger up yelling obscenities…

A couple of days later I underline what I am reading – '…Everything that touches me comes through the hand of my Heavenly Father who continues to love me, who continues to maintain control of my life, who continues to be totally responsible for my life as he does with all His created things….'

I would not wish to relive my life over again. I would not wish my griefs to be experienced by another, not even my worst enemy.

Yet if that level of brokenness experienced over a lifetime was the only way to know God, my Lord, Saviour and Friend, as I now know Him within a personal relationship I can only eagerly yet with fear, shout three words… "Bring it on!"

Contact information
At this writing Lisa Denny has authored two books:

The Making Of A Jewel
The Diaries. A Testimony of One Rescued from the Pit

Order your copies of Lisa's books today
All are available through Amazon,
Barnes and Noble, Books-A-Million,
and wherever fine Christian books are sold.

Rev. John P. Harris
When Dreams Are Dashed

There are times in some people's lives when God's grace does not appear as a quiet gentle voice in the wind. There are times, like my life for instance, when God throws a stick of dynamite into your life and blows the whole thing up. And that is exactly what happened to me. The explosion was so violent it also blew open my wife's life. Some of the debris was scattered throughout the church where we served. It even hit my daughter, who was living in Connecticut at the time, and some of my siblings. Grace for me was violent! But the process of God breathing new life into me and my wife over the next three years was more beautiful and extraordinary than I have ever experienced in my entire life.

--- Commentary / John Dee Jeffries ---

Many people struggle to move forward in life! At some point they seem to make forward progress! Then, inexplicably, the long arm of the past grabs them and pulls them backward! They're suddenly overwhelmed and stymied. Deep feelings of guilt, shame, regret and more become their constant companions! These dark feelings swirl within then rush to the surface – they're shattered – and stuck!

Into our Shattered Lives Jesus "restores" our Hearts! Into our Shattered Families Jesus "restores' our Homes! Into our Shattered World Jesus "restores" our Hope!

When we look backward at some of the situations we have been involved in or some of the choices we have made, we think, if only I had a second chance. Sometimes when we make a mistake in life it feels so final, you may think it's all over but, know this – God is a God who provides that much needed second chance. There's a new day coming! Our past failures are not final and our pain need not be fatal! Know this -- your yesterdays don't always have to determine your tomorrows!

When Dreams Are Dashed
Rev. John P. Harris

Hope deferred makes the heart sick...
                          Proverbs 13:12a NIV

No one ever says when they are a kid, "I want to be an addict when I grow up." We are just kids, and we dream about being doctors, writers, dancers, firemen or movie stars. Me, I wanted to be a cowboy.

But as time goes on life happens. For many young people life is good; for others, not so good. Some kids grow up in safe, loving environments, shielded by affirming and nurturing relationships. Other kids see, hear, and experience hardships. Unknowingly, the good and the not so good experiences of life begin to form and shape character. These character shaping forces and factors, unseen by the natural eye, determine who we are and who we are to become. And sometimes, being an addict is exactly what we end up becoming.

By the time I was ten years old the dream of being a cowboy faded and dreams of just not feeling lonely, abandoned, or bullied took center stage. I was the youngest of ten children and one of the younger kids in the neighborhood. There was very little supervision from my parents, or the other kid's parents. We were left to fend for and police ourselves most days. These circumstances created some very hard and frightful times in my daily life.

When I was five years old I was molested by my neighbors twelve-year-old son. At about the same time in my life, my good friend was being molested by his uncle. My friend would then teach me the things he experienced with his uncle, both of us thinking the actions were just a games boys played. It was all very hush-hush and no one ever discovered what was going on, but the introduction to sex at such an early age would fuel my desire for further exploration for the next forty-five years.

For the first ten years of my life I hardly knew my dad. He was a hardworking man who was seldom home.

He also was a heavy drinker. In 1973 my dad lost his job. Our family went from upper middle class to barely making ends meet. Everything seemed to happen so quickly. This was a major factor that molded my character and shaped my emotions. For the first time in my life my dad was home a lot -- and he was not a nice man. He was an angry, bitter man and was drunk all the time.

Because our financial situation and my dad's inability to find meaningful employment for long stretches of time, my mother had to get a full time job for the first time in my young life. This left me home with my three older sisters. For some reason my sisters thought it was fun to verbally abuse and belittle me. This happened nearly every day of the week for nearly two years. The teasing and needling would go on and on and on until I burst out screaming or broke down in tears. It was a dreadful and humiliating time in my life. It only came to an end when I reached puberty, when I put on several pounds and grew several inches in the summer of 1976. One day I discovered I could defend myself by physically lashing out at the girls. It was not long after that their terrorizing ended. But those two years of abuse added to my already twisted feelings of insecurity and fear.

THE WIDE GATE
"wide is the gate and broad is the way that leads to destruction," Matthew 7:13b NIV

I didn't know it at the time, but everyone has basic needs. There is a saying in the therapeutic world: all needs must be met; all needs will be met. In the early part of my life my need for affection, acceptance, and assurance were not being met in a natural nurturing environment, so they were replaced by experimenting with drugs and sex, and by pretending I was anyone expect who I felt I actually was.

By my early teens I was well on my way to a very confusing and destructive time in my life. For the most part my daily routines looked pretty much like every other teenager's life; school days and summertime adventures, bonding with friends, and falling in and out of love more than once or twice. But everything I did, and everywhere I went I realize now that I was never fully myself. My ongoing and underlying fear was that if people really knew me they wouldn't love or accept me; primarily because I didn't really like myself.

I started smoking cigarettes and pot at ten years of age. The first time I got drunk was eleven. By the summer of 1975, at twelve years old I was experimenting with LSD and pills that I was stealing from my neighbor's medicine cabinets. The alcohol and drugs brought out a persona that felt very comfortable being boisterous and fun loving, and a little dangerous. There was always a reason to party and joke and laugh and play. But I never wanted to be too committed or to invested into any one thing, or allow people to recognize my underlying feelings. I was a master of masks, masquerade and smoke-and-mirrors.

At age fourteen I started sneaking into bars and attending all the high school keg parties. I went to quite a few keg parties, quite a few. I was drinking nearly every weekend and smoking pot every day.

I had my first serious girlfriend at fifteen, which was a great boost to my ego. But, just as most young relationships go, we eventually broke up. My heart was broken and the rejection was overwhelming, so in order to cope I handled it the only way I knew how, I increased my intake of alcohol and drugs to drown the pain.

I was sixteen at the beginning of my senior year in high school. I was a party animal to say the least, but in some strange turn of events I was elected as Senior class President. I certainly was not your prototypical class president; I wasn't a popular jock or one of the smartest students grade wise. But I did pledge to throw some great parties, and for some crazy reason the campaign worked.

I must admit, between the extra attention at school, the parties I was throwing, and the fact that my new girlfriend graduated two years before me and was one of the most popular girls in town, I was on a pretty decent roll in the ego department for my senior year.

In the fall of 1980 I was introduced to cocaine. The first time I snorted it was at a party with my girlfriend. One of her friends was laying out lines on a mirror and asked me if I wanted to try some. I didn't know the large pile sitting in the mirror was for portioning out and snorted the whole pile. One would think I would have gotten sick as a dog, but something worse happened; I feel in love the drug.

As exhilarating as my senior year of high school was, the old adage of what goes up must come down rang true in due time. I graduated in June of 1981 and by the end of the summer my girlfriend broke up with me. Losing two very important ego boosters seemingly all at once was devastating. Without anywhere else to turn I went on a party binge. Cocaine was a regular part of my daily routine. I was either snorting it, or finding ways to get it.

I also found an outlet for my broken heart by swearing off women for a spell. But my desire to still feel satisfied needed to be fed.

I soon discovered how to meet other men anomalously for sex. I didn't date any of them, in fact I barely knew many of their names, but for those brief few moments the need to feel gratified was filled. Over time I begin to feel very guilty and ashamed of what I was doing. Even though lots of people were exploring their sexuality during the eighties, inwardly I felt that what I was doing was wrong, inappropriate. The guilt and shame often felt overwhelming, and I would secretly carry these feelings for a very long time.

Years earlier, at age twelve, I discovered that I had a knack for cooking and I quickly developed some marketable skills. I had the opportunity in my early years to work with some very good chefs. Eventually I decided to try my hand at being a chef. At eighteen, after I completed high school, I applied to the Culinary Institute of America but, I did not have the money to attend. So, I joined the Army in 1983 in hopes of raising the funds through the GI Bill.

Unfortunately, my originals plans went sideways when I starting dating my daughters mother in the fall of 1984. We were young and passionately infatuated with each other. We were married within six months of our first date. A few months later, my daughter was born.

Time passed.

By age twenty-two I was a husband and a father with a baby. I was still in the Army and living in Germany. The pace of life was hectic. My addictions increased. I was in way over my head. Unfortunately, instead of slowing down on the partying it only picked up. I had no clue on how to be a husband and a father and it showed. Although I loved my wife and child very much, I acted more like a frat pledge than a man. I was ill equipped to fulfill my vows, and my wife felt lonely and rejected. She soon found someone else to help meet her needs. I filed for divorce in 1988. The marriage was officially over by January 1990.

CLIFF HANGING
The way of fools seems right to them, Proverbs 12:15a NIV

At twenty-seven, I was a broken and demoralized guy. I had lost my wife, never pursued my dream of attending the CIA, was barely making a living, and partying way too hard. I felt rejected, small, and useless. I saw myself as a failure and hated the way I felt nearly all time. Worse yet, I saw no way to change. I reckoned it would be best to act like nothing bothered me in the least, pursue my compulsion for hard drugs and parties, and satiate my physical needs through illicit sex and pornography.

In the summer of 1991 I was introduced to what eventually would be my downfall; crack cocaine. I was hosting a wild party at my mom & dads house while they were away on vacation. I honestly didn't know half the people there, and many of them were not even of legal age to be drinking. It was late in the night, the hallucinogenic I had taken earlier were still in full effect, but the party had tempered down to just a few people. One of my friends asked if she could use my bedroom for a while. Curious as to why, I said yes but only if I could join her. I did not have a clue what I was about what we were going to do and I had no idea about what was going to happen.

Once behind the closed door, I was began smoking cocaine. With that first hit I knew I was in trouble. As intense and euphoric as the high was, I did not realize that crack cocaine would slowly but violently destroy my whole life.

In spite of my partying and crazy lifestyle, I was always captivated by politics. Social justice causes, fair labor laws, and the environmental concerns were issues that were important to me.

In early 1992 I volunteered to work on a Presidential candidate's campaign. I started by helping with a few local events in my home state of Connecticut, but soon found myself helping out in Vermont and New York. By the end of April, I had caught the political bug big time.

While chatting one night in a campaign office with some of the volunteers and the candidate, I mentioned that I wanted to run for office someday. Several others also expressed their desire to get more involved. The candidate, in passing I am sure, said we should all do just that. "go home and run for something" were the words I am fairly sure he said. So I did just that.

In May of 1992, with no financial means or any support from the democratic party, I throw my hat in the ring for the 36th house district of Connecticut. It was perhaps the boldest thing I have ever done, and I enjoyed the political race immensely. I didn't win the election, but I came very close. So close in fact, that the party took notice.

During the following election I managed the campaign for the eventual winner of the house seat. I was elected as the Party Chairman in my home town and was elected to a few local boards as well. Nevertheless, I was still living a double life, and my addiction to crack was out of control.

SAVED BY GRACE
But God demonstrates his own love for us in this: While we were still sinners, Christ died for us. Romans 5:8 NIV

In the summer of 1995 the most amazing thing happened in my life; I was saved! My brother-in-law started bringing me to church for a few months. He invited me to attend a Christian concert. I initially though that it was a crazy theatrical show. However, by the end of the concert there was an altar call. I responded. I asked God for His forgiveness. Though I did not know it at the time, that pivotal moment had a profound impact on the rest of my life.

Up until this point in my life I was fairly happy go lucky when it came to my drug abuse and lifestyle. I had never been in trouble with the police and rarely had trouble when making purchases or hustling to get my drugs. All of that changed once I started confessing that I was born again believer and a child of God. For awhile I started straddling the fence. I continued to try and live the same addictive, criminally insane life as I had as I had lived before I was saved. Spiritual road blocks, obstacles and barriers to my old drug lifestyle began popping up all over the place, everywhere.

As if on command it seemed that the streets became more and more dangerous. I was mugged for my drug money. More than once a thug with a gun or a knife stuck it in my face. People broke into and stole from my home all the time. One day in particular, a friend took all my drugs, my car and my money while I was crashed out from days of drugging. When I woke up and realized what happened, it took me days to recover the car, but the drugs and money were gone for good. I also became increasingly paranoid. I was constantly plagued with anxious thoughts that people were watching me or devising plans to get me.

Knowing I was not able to continue with my insane double life for much longer, I stepped down as Party Chairman at the end of 1996. I then moved to a different town in hopes of staying under the radar.

Six months later, while working for a longtime friend, I was fired from my job – embezzlement. I had embezzled money from the company. My employer filed a complaint with the local police department. I was called in for questioning. Although no charges were filed by my employer, during the interview it came out that I was addicted to crack. The police immediately started surveilling me, and within a few months I was arrested for the possession of crack cocaine and operating a drug factory out of my home.

When I was arrest in early 1997, my daily crack addiction escalated. It was literally killing me. I would not sleep for days on end, my teeth were falling out, and I weighed so little you could see the outline of my cheeks and ribs. I was dying; spiritually, emotionally, and physically.

With nowhere else to turn, I cried out to my Pastor for help. The day after my 34th birthday, December 12, 1997, he dropped me off at a yearlong Christian ministry for drug addicts (Teen Challenge). He instructed me to complete the program and to not leave the Teen Challenge ministry until God said I was to leave. Six years later I was still there; saved, sober, ordained, and serving as a director in the ministry. God demonstrated His grace and His favor on me.

Relational issues and problems that I had never dealt with began to surface: the feelings of loneliness, abandonment, or of being bullied. Although my bondage to drugs and alcohol was broken, I still wrestled with sexual addictions. I was no longer addicted to drugs. I never stopped feeding my addiction to sex. I discovered internet pornography and chat rooms. They were the vehicles I used to satisfy and strengthen my growing sexual cravings.

In 2003 I felt it was time to move on from Teen Challenge. Even while living a double life, I thought for sure God would instantly open a door for me to Pastor a church in spite of the fact that I had no pastoral experience. Over the next two years I submitted my resume to several churches, but the opportunity did not materialize. In my frustration I concluded that perhaps God was through using me in ministry, I once again found myself feeling alone and abandoned. For nearly two years I floundered, without any real direction in my life. I never returned to drugs, but my sexual appetite grew as I found myself more and more isolated than ever.

In late 2006 I was stirred to straighten out my life and make a push to get back into fulltime ministry. While attending a Christian music festival I sat in on one of the featured speaker's sessions. Throughout his talk I felt as if he was speaking directly to me. I don't remember the whole topic but I clearly remember him stating "While you wait for God to move in your life ask yourself, what am I doing for God?" That question hit me like a ton of bricks. I returned home determined to return to ministry, but I knew I had to clean up my sinful lifestyle. It was hard and took several months but I begin to resist the daily sexual temptations.

By the summer of 2007 I decided I could now get back into ministry and started to apply for positions around the country. Ironically, I landed back in Teen Challenge. I was sure that Teen Challenge is where I was called to serve. I was determined to refrain from any sexual sin while I ministered.

After only a few months at Teen Challenge, something totally unexpected happened. On January 1, 2008 I met my soon to be wife. A relationship was the furthest thing from my mind at the time, but once we were dating I knew I was in love. On June 21, 2008 we were married.

Unfortunately, my position did not last long at Teen Challenge, but it didn't matter. I was convinced God had cleaned me up to meet my wife, not land me back in ministry.

In 2009 my wife and I decided to move to Tampa, Florida. She felt she wanted to leave the corporate life and return to fulltime ministry. Since I had a financially stable job that allowed me the freedom of working from home the plan seemed perfect.

Within just a few months of searching she landed a position as a Worship Pastor at a local church in Tampa. It was a great opportunity for her, but her job was very demanding, and the hours were long. I found myself with way too much time on my hands. The idle time provided opportunities for me to resume watching pornography. Once I gave in to the temptation to watch pornography, it didn't take too long before I started chatting with people on line and eventually started meeting people for sex.

The guilt and shame were overwhelming. I had

convinced myself that being married would fix me. It did not! In 2012 I was offered the Executive Pastors Job at the same church my wife was serving. I quickly accepted the opportunity as being a Pastor had been my hope since 2003. In addition, I foolishly thought that that would be the deterrent I needed to overcome my addiction. It was not! In fact, my addiction grew worse as the guilt and shame compounded.

For nearly fourteen years, 2000 – 2014, with only brief periods of abstinence, I led a double life. Pastor, dad and husband on one side; secretive sex addict on the other. I seemingly mastered the ability to separate my two lives into compartments. When I was behind a pulpit or spending time with my family I was fully invested into being the man of God I was striving to be. When I was alone and separated from my family and church I was fully absorbed into the dark world of pornography and risky sexual encounters.

The shame and the self-loathing were heavy, but the call of my addiction loomed large. I thought for sure I would go to my grave without ever being free from my brokenness. I convinced myself that if anyone ever found out I would be outcast and rejected by those I depended on for love and validation. I was in a no win situation and convinced myself that it was my cross to bear, or the thorn I would have to suffer alone.

Shock Wave

There will be trouble and distress for every human being who does evil, Romans 2:9a NIV

While my wife and I were still serving on staff at the church, it was revealed to my Senior Pastor that I was looking for sex partners online. As a result, both my wife and I were fired from our jobs at the church; me for being a broken sex addict, her for being an addict's wife. I fully understood why I needed to step down, but the way she was treated was not fair in any manner. The reality was, the church leadership was ill equipped to manage such an explosive scandal in the church and they did not have the programs or experience to minister to our brokenness. They thought they were doing what was best for the flock and the image of the church. Nonetheless, their decision to not help us left my wife and I completely isolated and vulnerable.

The news of my porn addiction and extra marital affairs nearly destroyed my wife emotionally and spiritually, and our marriage was on the brink of collapse. I was an emotional wreck and I would be lying if I did not confess the thought of suicide briefly passed through my head on a few occasions. I did not think I would ever be forgiven by my wife. I was convinced I had wounded her so deeply that she might not ever recover. She later told me that I did not hold that much power over her, as her trust and strength were in the Lord. But I was not capable of understanding any of that while in the midst of our crises.

My wife and I found ourselves in a very desperate situation. We no longer had a church to assist us, and many of our friends did not know how to emotionally support us. We were desperate to get away from Tampa and to get help for our shattered emotions. While reaching out to a local counselor for some initial help, he told us about a ministry specializing in helping sex addicts and their families recover from the damage of addiction; HopeQuest Ministry Group, Inc. Desperate and with nowhere else to turn, we made a call to the ministry. They offered to enroll us in their group ministries; Walking Free for men with sexual addictions, and Journey, a healing ministry for the wives of addicts. They also helped us enroll in weekly individual and marriage counseling.

NEW LIFE
Before I was afflicted I went astray, but now I obey your word. Psalm 119:67 NIV

On April 25, 2014 we packed up our apartment in Tampa, FL and moved to Woodstock, GA. It was a time of great unknowing for both of us. For the first time in our marriage we were not sure of what was going to happen in the future. We had no plans beyond making it to the next counseling session or attending the next group meeting. We had no friends around us for support, and neither of us even knew if our marriage was going to survive.

The process of recovery would be long and very emotional. There were many challenges to overcome as both my wife and I worked through the wounds of betrayal. We also received spiritual and emotional healing from other scars inflicted on us from a history of hard times in our lives.

I want everyone reading this story to know, there are times in some people's lives when God's grace does not appear as a quiet gentle voice in the wind. There are times, like my life for instance, when God throws a stick of dynamite into your life and blows the whole thing up. And that is exactly what happened to me. The explosion was so violent it also blew open my wife's life. Some of the debris was scattered throughout the church where we served. It even hit my daughter, who was living in Connecticut at the time, and some of my siblings. Grace for me was violent! But the process of God breathing new life into me and my wife over the next three years was more beautiful and extraordinary than I have ever experienced in my entire life.

In spite of my wife not being able to work for several months immediately after all my sexual sin was revealed, and me losing my job working from home and having to take another job making half of my pay, we never missed paying a monthly bill. There were days that people we didn't even know would hand us an envelope full of cash to help us buy groceries or put gas in our cars; the church we were attending helped us with food and paid a few utilities bills for us when we first arrived in Woodstock; one kind soul gave me a blank check to fix both our cars. The bill came to nearly four thousand dollars and he still insisted we write out the check for five thousand dollars so we would have some reserve cash in the bank. Miracle after miracle happened throughout our time of seeking help. And the most important miracle of all was the work God did in my, and my wife's hearts, and the work he did in our marriage.

Today I am extremely grateful to report, that after three years and countless hours of prayer, counseling, and communion with others experiencing similar trials, we have a new marriage based on trust and authenticity, and we are more in love than we were before our entire world blew up.

Best of all, God has healed decades of unmet and abused needs through His grace, love and guidance. My wife and I have a deeper understanding of how we ended up where were in our emotional lives; and how to take responsibility and allow forgiveness to free us from the wounds life left us with. Today I can truly say I am free, and God has been amazingly good to me.

Contact Information

John and his wife are now on staff at *HopeQuest Ministry Group*. In addition to providing the free support groups of *Walking Free and Journey*, they also offer a twelve-week residential treatment program for adults with substance abuse and/or sexual brokenness.

If you are anyone you know is in need of assistance, or would like to start a local *Walking Free* or *Journey group* in your area, email John or visit the ministry website.

john.harris@hopequestgroup.org
https://hopequestgroup.org/

John Dee Jeffries
A Dark Companion -- Defeated

"We talked about death. The husband and I, we talked about it! We did! I always thought," says she, "I always thought about our death in a sort of romantic kind of way. I thought that when death came for one of us, well, the one that died first would sort of pass 'gently into the night.' But, when he died, well, there was nothing 'gentle' about it....and, there was nothing romantic about it. His death was hard. Long. Drawn out. Messy. And...."

At some point everyone feels the fear of death. No one is immune. Fear of death, however, can actually paralyze a person – grip and hold.

Can we conquer our fear of death? It depends on who the "we" is referred to in this question.

A Dark Companion -- Defeated
John Dee Jeffries

Smile

11:30 p.m.

"Can you come?" says the voice on the other end of the phone. "He won't make it through the night!" Thirty minutes later we met in the front room of her home. A hospital bed filled the room. On it was a man, her husband. Tubes, wires, and machines were everywhere.

"He's not saved," says she. "And he's going to die tonight!"

"One other thing," says she. He's completely paralyzed. He can't talk or move – he can't even squeeze your hand or finger."

I bent over the hospital bed and began sharing Christ, slowly whispering God's plan of salvation into his ear. I closed my share time with him by leading him in that special prayer of faith and repentance, urging him to invite Christ into what remained of his life.

"Do you think he invited Christ into his life," says she. "I'm going to try to find out," says I.

"Mister, I know you can't talk and I know you can't even squeeze my hand, but I noticed while we were praying that your lip quivered and moved, just a tad. Sir, if you invited Christ into your life – if you can, would you smile.!"

Unbelievably, he flashed one of the biggest, sweetest smiles I think I'd ever seen. Before sunrise, he died. I call him the man who smiled his way into heaven.

Sometimes, things seem hopeless. Sometimes, it seems as if all is lost. The key word is "seems" – what "seems" to be is not always what is. The world of appearances is often deceptive. So, be patient. Trust God….. and smile!

The Angel Of Death!

"Come, please! Please come! Come before night!"

His voice was frantic, filled with fright – fearful! He and his wife had attended but not joined our church years earlier, and, now – they were in a thick of trouble!

"I don't know if she's insane or on the verge of insanity – but something's wrong! Come, please! Please come! Come before night!"

Later – mid-afternoon – I went to their home. I saw her before she saw me! I was at the bottom of a curved stairwell as she carefully and cautiously started down. She had aged since I'd last seen her.

She was startled when she first saw me! Instinctively, she drew a quick, deep breath and just as quickly drew her hand to her chest! Then – her eyes – she was dealing with a greater fear!

"What are you looking for," says I?

"He's not here yet," says she. "They say he comes at night! But, you never know! He may come tonight! He may not. You never know!"

She spoke hesitantly about her fears, about her anxieties and about a little graveyard next to an abandoned white clapboard church, the church of her childhood.

"I must get out of here, while it is day. I must, I must have fresh air!"

Centuries ago, Christians sometimes celebrated a

believer's death as his "birthday" – their day of entry into heaven! They celebrated because they believed what the Bible had to say about death, i.e., Christ has delivered His children from the fear of death – and we no longer need to live in bondage to that fear (Hebrews 2:14-15). The early Christians understood (and believed) that "death had no sting and the grave had no victory!" (1 Corinthian 15:55).

A broken moon peered through two large oaks in front of their home. A flush of pink and red azaleas danced as gentle twisting winds blew. It was later that night. I had returned, as promised. She was on her couch, which was strategically placed so that she could see both the front and back first floor entrances to her home. She had somehow come to believe that when the Angel of Death came – he would come through either the front or back entrance. She had so positioned herself that if he came in the front, she would escape through the back; and vice versa.

She disbelieved Scripture – disregarded its sufficiency – and rejected all attempts to help her. I lost touch with them and never heard from them in the aftermath of hurricane Katrina.

Question: What about you? What about me? Can we conquer our fear of death? Everyone must eventually battle fear! Some fear heights. Others fear flying. Still others fear drowning, or snakes, or mice. Everyone has a fear of death. No one is immune. Fear of death, however, can actually paralyze a person – grip and hold us -- such as the lady who feared the Angel of Death.

Can we conquer our fear of death? Again, it depends on who the "we" is referred to in this question.

If you are numbered with the unsaved, the lost and you are not born again -- you should fear death. As written in

Hebrews 10:31, "It is a fearful thing to fall into the hands of the living God."

If you are numbered with the saved, the redeemed and you are born again – you have nothing to fear. David understood that he had nothing to fear when he wrote, "Even though I walk through the valley of the shadow of death, I will fear no evil, for you are with me." (Psalm 23:4) Paul understood this too. He writes to young Timothy (and to you – and to me). He wants us to know that "…God has not given us a spirit of fear…"

Paul could sleep peacefully, night or day, with the thought that the Angel of Death could come for him at any time… And you can sleep peacefully too! And so can I! And so can that lady – through faith in and assurance from Christ! He is our peace!

A Dark Companion – Defeated!

"We talked about death. The husband and I, we talked about it! We did! I always thought," says she, "I always thought about our death in a sort of romantic kind of way. I thought that when death came for one of us, well, the one that died first would sort of pass 'gently into the night.' But, when he died, well, there was nothing 'gentle' about it….and, there was nothing romantic about it. His death was hard. Long. Drawn out. Messy. And…."

Thinking about her and the tragic death of her husband led me to think about a time when I was not yet a man, yet, I was no longer a child. It was one of those strange times when I thought I knew it all. I was driving dad's car through City Park with Genny, my future wife, seated in the passenger seat. As I recall we were somewhere near the City Park golf course in New Orleans.

Its seared in my memory -- a golfer was taking a swing at his ball when suddenly, into my line of sight came the image of a man – putting a gun to his head – and pulling the trigger!

As the golfer dropped his club to run toward the afflicted man, I pulled the car to the side of the road and ran to see if I could help.

From a few feet away, the dying man looked like a fallen tree. His body was facedown. He was dead less than a minute. The golfer and I stood there, side by side, looking at him. Neither of us knew what to do. Then there was a sudden twitching, a quiver in the dead flesh of the man as he lay there.

"He's alive! He's alive! My God, he's still alive," shouted the golfer. Shock ran through me as the dying man's head turned toward us. His small closed eyes suddenly opened. He looked at us – then collapsed one final time and died!

Thinking about the death of this husband, and thinking about the self-inflicted death of the man near the golf course, well, there was nothing 'gentle' about either…. and, there was nothing romantic about death either. Both death's were hard. One was long, drawn out and messy. The other was quick, messy and….

My stomach churned. The golfer threw up. We wept.

--- 000 ---

Two thousand years ago Jesus attended a funeral – the funeral of a friend. He spoke. Before He spoke, however,

He did something. "Jesus wept," says the fisherman, John, who attended the funeral. "Jesus wept."

Jesus was not powerless nor was He helpless when He encountered death that day – yet, He wept. Jesus wept because death had intruded into yet another family – and snatched someone loved, deeply loved, from that family.

Listen! Death has never been, is not now, nor will it ever be the plan of God. Open your Bible to the book of Genesis and you encounter God as He is – He is the God of Life! He speaks and this place is teeming with life. He speaks and hearts begin to 'thump' -- Life-giving blood begins to coarse through veins and lungs begin to…. Because God is the God of Life!

Then, tragically, sin came into the world and with it a dark companion – death! The mystery of iniquity began to unfold. Sin, like an inherited disease – a terminal disease – is passed from generation to generation -- and we all have it! We all sin! We all die! God hated death so much that He "gave His only begotten Son [so] that whosoever believeth on Him should not perish but have everlasting life!"

Why? Because God is a God of life!

Thanatophobia, or fear of death, is a rather complicated *phobia*. Most people are afraid of dying. Some fear being dead, while others fear the actual act of dying. If fear of death affects your day-to-day affairs then you might have *thanatophobia.*

Morbid, obsessive feelings and fears about death are, for many people, rooted in religious beliefs. These feelings and fears are more powerful and intense when a person is experiencing religious uncertainty. These obsessive fears often lead those afflicted to withdraw from God – thereby intensifying that sense of the absence of God.

When a person approaches the time of their death or the death of a loved one, frightful feelings and fears may also surface.

Death may be sensationalized in our culture. It may be glamorized in the movies. We may even carry romantic images about our own death and the death of people we love dearly! Death is not our friend! I repeat – Death is not our friend! Death is a foe!

And, Jesus said, "Rejoice! I have overcome…." Sin's dark companion – Death – has been defeated! Death has no sting! Death has no victory!

Rejoice! Life eternal, life everlasting -- that is the heritage and inheritance that is available through Christ! And a glorious, ultimate destiny that is beyond our ability to comprehend….

Myra Jean Myers
'Oh GOD, I Have Murdered!'

A year and a-half later, I felt a crushing weight of grief and guilt – devastating pain: I knew beyond the shadow of a doubt – I was responsible for the death of my child –

'Oh GOD, I have murdered'!

For four decades, I have regretted believing the Lies: It is not a child - yet; after all, it is legal - it must be okay.

--- Commentary / John Dee Jeffries ---

In the shadows – near the rough edge of ministry – every pastor hears the faint echo of yesterday and he sees the fading faces of those who languished in the darker valleys of life.

Many years ago a man named John was forced to deal with a tragedy that was far greater than he could bear. The wounds of life, the wounds of love – and a pain so deep, so very, very deep, and so great – these were flung upon him. A large commercial airliner fell out of the sky on his home. He suffered the death of his young daughter. She was a child, his precious child.

The wounds of life, the wounds of love – Sometimes they inflict a pain so deep, so very, very severe, and so great that poets and philosopher's and others who think deeply about such things are stunned to silence.

But, what if the wounds that caused such grief were self-inflicted? What if the long finger of guilt, shame and sorrow, what if that finger was pointed at you. What then?

Abortion Hurts Everyone
Myra Jean Myers

Like millions of women, I made the tragic, devastating, 'poor-choice' of abortion -- as a married woman. In January 1973 at the age of 28, I informed my husband that I was pregnant with our sixth child. This time, he said there was only one thing to do – abortion, which had been legalized the week before.

We had never considered abortion during the previous pregnancies – not even when I was a single college senior in 1965 – it wasn't legal. Instead, we married.

How did we go from understanding, knowing that pregnant is to be with child to – It is not a child, yet? Deception! We were deceived by the U.S. Supreme Court ruling, Roe vs. Wade, and Planned Parenthood.

The clerk at Planned Parenthood said nothing about pregnancy, the abortion procedure, risks or consequences.

She did say, "If you have trouble with it afterwards, we have counseling available". WHY would I have any trouble with it? I wondered. She made an appointment for me for the following Saturday.

The night before my appointment to abort I was not a Christian but I asked, "GOD, is there anything wrong with what I am going to do? Man says it isn't even life. What do YOU say?"

In the morning, a clerk called from the abortion facility to tell me, "The doctor has to cancel his appointments this morning. What do you want to do?" I did not remember the night before; I did not make the connection. I wasn't listening – to GOD! I asked my husband what he wanted to do. "How about next Saturday?" he asked.

Co-dependent, I made another appointment!

In the waiting room, I could hear the conversation of two other women: "It is our second – too soon." "It is our third – we only want two." I thought nothing; I felt nothing – Denial.

Lying on the abortionist's table, I didn't remember being in this position five times previously - as I birthed my children.

A year and a-half after the abortion, I felt a crushing weight of grief and guilt – devastating pain: I knew beyond the shadow of a doubt – I was responsible for the death of my child – 'Oh GOD, I have murdered'!

For four decades, I have regretted believing the Lies: It is not a child - yet; after all, it is legal - it must be okay. Like tens of millions of women and men in the USA and 40-50 million each year around the world, we failed to realize that we had become mothers and fathers at fertilization.

In 1968, our third child was born two months premature

and died. Of course the loss of a child brought grief, but not the compounded grief plus guilt of being responsible for the death and loss of a child as I was through making the tragic, 'poor-choice' of abortion.

Abortion had destroyed our parent-child relationship and nearly destroyed our marriage due to the grief, guilt, shame and the blaming. Our marriage is among the few to survive. Within one to five years following abortion, 70-90% of relationships between the women and men dissolve.

Nothing wounds women and men like taking the life of your own child! Today my husband and I agree: "Had abortion been illegal, we would not have aborted our child!" (nor lost his future children, our grandchildren) "Abortion should never have been legalized".

Abortion has also affected my life even to this day through the damage of the unsafe abortion procedure, resulting in a hysterectomy shortly afterwards at the age of 28 – followed by estrogen deprivation and its impact.

Grief and guilt are synonymous with abortion. There is a natural grief because of loss through death, but also a compounded grief because of personal responsibility in the death and loss -guilt. There are no words to describe the crushing weight of guilt I felt October 14, 1974. As I felt the weight, I knew the truth – 'Oh GOD, I have murdered'!

The Peace that replaced the weight was greater… Forgiveness and a right Relationship with GOD. For forty-two years now and for eternity I will be forever grateful for the weight of conviction that brought my acknowledgment of the truth! And the Joy of knowing I am the mother of six children – not only of the four I was raising, but also of the one who died from premature birth and the one I had aborted - they are already with HIM. What a reunion is waiting for me!

JESUS understands: HE bore our sin and carried our sorrows. "Before I formed you in the womb, I Knew you. You were in MY Care before you were born." "All have gone astray, turning each one, his/her own way." "There is none good, no not one. None that seeks after GOD." "I Have Loved you with an Everlasting Love; therefore, with Lovingkindness I have drawn you." "Herein is Love, not that we have loved GOD but that HE has Loved us and given HIS SON to make atonement for our sins." "For GOD did not send HIS SON into the world to condemn the world, but that the world (you and I) through HIM might be saved." "He who has the SON has the LIFE; he who does not have the SON does not have the LIFE." "Come unto ME, all who are weary and heavy burdened and I Will give you Rest. Take MY Yoke upon you and learn from ME and I Will give you Rest for your souls." "To as many as Receive HIM, JESUS gives the Power, the Right to become Children of GOD." "Whosoever will, may come…and whosoever comes, I Will Not turn away."

What if the wounds that caused such grief were self-inflicted? What if the long finger of guilt, shame and sorrow, what if that finger was pointed at us. What then?

Helpful Information

Every day of every month the loss of life due to the Deception of legalized abortion adversely impacts the women, men, families. 1 of every 4 - in our families, among our friends, in the Church, communities. Everyone needs forgiveness! Help those impacted by abortion by referring them to the:...

www.internationalhelplineforabortionrecovery.org

Everyone can be a part of restoring the protection and respect for all life by making available the legal Declarations of testimony for women and men who have experienced the devastating harm of abortion. Available:

www.operationoutcry.org
Touch Hearts, Change Lives, Restore Justice!

Contact Information
Myra Jean Myers

Myra Myers is a National Advisor to Operation Outcry. Check out Myra J Myers Photo Biography/Operation Outcry and YouTube Gospel Testimony: Myra's Story - Abortion Hurts Everyone.

http://www.youtube.com/user/myoomy1
https://vimeo.com/myramyers/abortionhurtseveryone
http://www.youtube.com/user/myoomy1

Brenda Stephens
Dark Winter's Night

--- Commentary / John Dee Jeffries ---

It's every little girls life-long dream. A Cinderella fantasy. Wedding day bells. Prince Charming. Two magic words – *"I Do."* A dreamy little cottage with a white picket fence. And, they lived *happily ever after*....or do they.

What happens when they don't? Christian author Brenda Stephens has put together a powerfully-written, profound book – *Dark Winter's Night*. Brenda's story is a raw, soul-wrenching glimpse into the darkness of divorce. Through circumstances beyond her control Brenda walked through the darkness of divorce, not once, not twice, but three times. Brenda writes with a sensitive honesty that leads through the darkness of divorce into God's glorious light.

Dark Winter's Night
Brenda Stephens

"Help me Lord," I cried. "It is too much. I can't do this. I can't be a single parent. There is no way," my mind rebelled. "I can't be both Mom and Dad. I can't pay all the bills, keep the house clean, buy the groceries, do laundry, maintain the car and computer, discipline the kids, help with homework, spend time with the kids, go to church, do good news club, do sleepovers and I couldn't do anything else that my mind didn't conjure up in that moment of panic. When would I have time for you, Lord, or any moment for me?

HELP, LORD! HELP!

----- 000 -----

Broken promises always seemed to play a big part in my life. They started with my dad then worked their way through each of my husbands. This created an inner environment of doubt and disbelief. The result? I have a hard time believing when someone/anyone makes a promise. Lies have been a constant part of each of my marriages too. Consequently, when I hear that God is always truthful; and when I hear that God always keeps his promises – I have a hard time with that.

Yet, I keep hearing that God is always consistently truthful. And then I keep hearing that God won't break his promises! What is that? Even my earthy father broke his promises to me. In fact, he still does. So I don't have a lot of good examples of what keeping promises looks like. But I am willing to watch and learn.

My Prayer

Abba Father, I am willing to learn. I am willing to trust. I am willing to take you at your Word. I choose to believe that you do not lie. I choose to believe that you keep your promises. Your Word says that I should delight myself in you and you will give me the desires of my heart. I don't know what my heart desires right now, Lord, because you have so blessed my life these last few months. But you do. I do know, Lord, that I want complete reconciliation with my son. This is my hearts cries right now, Lord. And I'll hang on to the promises you have given me. In your precious holy name I pray, Amen

----- 000 -----

A sink full of dirty dishes, dirty diapers, toys and clothes everywhere, and me depressed for three weeks. Not a good combination.

"Lord is this what my life is now? Is this what the divorce has sentenced me to endure? An endless cycle of depression and guilt? And an endless mess that is never clean?"

No, because God is my Redeemer and depression is wrapped up in fear. And my Jesus has not given me a spirit of fear but of power, love, and a sound mind.

Will the pain of the divorce ever stop? Yes, because I know that "all things work together for good for those who love the Lord." (Romans 8:28) Nothing brings me greater comfort than knowing I have helped someone else get through a struggle.

My Prayer

Father, I hate when fear overcomes me. In those times, you come to me and comfort my heart, reminding me fear is not from you. I get caught up in the worldly things of how much I have to do, instead of focusing on you. Help me to prioritize my time and focus on things you want me to focus on.

----- ooo -----

How am I going to do this?

I was a very new, immature Christian. I hadn't grown a lot in the church I was attending. I did my best, my very best, to do all the things I knew to do. I was reading my Bible, going to church on Sunday, praying, and talking to my mom about things. But I had no idea how to do this single parenting thing -- and neither did she.

Mom had never been a single mom. She has been married to my Dad for 59 years now. I also had my best friend Russ. "Unka Russ" Meg called him. He'd been my best friend for 5 years, the best I could ask for. It didn't matter what time it was, I could call him and he would answer. He was always there for me. But still, even he didn't know what I was enduring. He had never been married and he didn't have children.

So I started crying out to God. Daily, sometimes hourly, persistently, I cried out to God. Asking, seeking and knocking, just like the Bible said. I believed the Bible was the living, breathing Word of God and everything it said was true. So I put it into practice. I cried out for a friend who knew what I was going through because my friend was going through it too. Here was someone who knew my sorrow, my struggles, my pain as a mom and my secret longings that went with being a woman.

And I cried out for God to give me strength to do the job He had called me to do. It wasn't until DeLayne (from here on out referred to as Layni) was 7 months that God brought us to a different church.

It was here, in this new church that I met so many people who poured into me. It was here I began to grow into the woman God wanted me to become. The first woman I met, who was part of the welcoming team, was Tamara. Turns out, she had been a single mom and knew my struggles. She offered to get coffee later in the week. I jumped on it. This would be the beginning of 7 of the most beautiful, wonderful, painful, stretching years I would ever know.

And God was behind every moment. Leading and guiding us all the way.

My Prayer

Daddy, For every woman who doesnt have a close friend or mentor to help them through this season, send them the very best there could be. Someone who can draw them closer to you.

----- 000 -----

Rejection

Psalms 91:14-16(NIV) For the Lord says "Because she loves me I will rescue her: I will make her great because she trusts in my name. When she calls on me I will answer; I will be with her in trouble and rescue her and honor her. I will satisfy her with a full life and give her my salvation.

Anger

All I feel is anger. What I thought were blessings from God are always taken away. Why? What am I doing wrong? I have so many struggles in my life. All my life I have been abandoned by the men in my life. Why can't I have love? No one has ever really stayed. Why do men always walk away from me. All I want is to be loved and cherished by someone for who I am. I don't want to hide who I am or become someone else. I just want to be authentic. I want to be real. Where do I go from here? How do I ever trust again?

My Prayer

Abba, I want to be satisfied. I want to feel your blessings. I want to understand why Your blessings come so hard for me. I have nowhere to turn but to you. I can't feel your love. I ask for that right now and I ask that You fill my heart to overflowing with Your peace and love. Fill my life with the good things that come from You. Redeem what the enemy has stolen from my life. In Your precious hands, I place my life, Amen.

----- 000 -----

Thrown Away

Damaged goods. I'm three times divorced now and that's what I see. Like a bruised melon no one wants. How is anyone going to want me after three men have thrown me away?

Is this how Jesus felt on the cross? He was rejected and thrown away by everyone. Even Peter, one of his most trusted disciples, denied even knowing him. But most hurtful had to be being rejected by God, His father. We think God rejected Him, how that must've hurt. But we must stop and think, His father rejected him, at the most painful point of his life. Yet, he didn't ask for any of it to stop. He completed the path set before him. His father welcomed Him home with open arms. Peter apologized, and some who had rejected him repented and accepted Him. Others didn't. Some never will.

So in the deepest point of our rejection, we can be sure Jesus knows and shares our pain and cries with us. He had victory over rejection and so will we.

My Prayer

Jesus, You know what I'm feeling. That gut wrenching pain I feel when I think I'm going to be rejected again. Thank you for Your comfort. Thank you that I can come to You and You know what I am feeling. Please be with me and help me with my insecurities. And for those reading this let them know they are not alone. Amen

A Little About Me

I was married the first time when I was 21. He was a violent, angry man I left after two years and two kids. I was single four years when I met my second husband. It was a whirlwind romance and we were married in less than three months. I don't recommend anyone do this. We lasted three years before he couldn't live with my bitterness anymore. Less than a year after the divorce was final I was married again to a man who was abusive and controlling and who molested my girls.

Now, seven years later, I am engaged to an amazing,

God-fearing man, who loves me for me, not for who he can make me into. I am scared but excited to start this journey.

May God bless you as richly as He has me.

Contact Information
Brenda Stephens

At this writing Brenda Stephens has authored one book…
DarkWinter's Night

Order your copy of Brenda's book today
It is available through Amazon,
Barnes and Noble, Books-A-Million,
and wherever fine Christian books are sold.

My Prayer

Lord, I pray for the women (and men) who are on the receiving end of someone else's hurtful free will -- And, feeling awful about it. I ask that you show them it has nothing to do with them. Show them that they are precious, worthy and valuable. Show them that You have a plan and a purpose for them beyond anything they could imagine. For those who will be going through a storm in the future, I pray that You start putting the supports in place now like You did for me. Show them how much You love them. I love you, Jesus, Amen

Dr. Jonathan Powell
But God Is Still Working

--- Commentary / John Dee Jeffries ---

Beneath the unfolding drama of history, God has His torchbearers, the shepherds of the new millennium. These are the strong nails that hold the church together. They are an assorted group, often ministering in obscurity – they are our pastors.

Some pastors are old. Some are young. Even now our pastors are shaping the future of the church and the nations in significant ways. They seek and long for, not a modern God made in the image of man, but the ancient God of Scripture, the God of Abraham, Isaac and Jacob, the God and Father revealed through the Son and confirmed in our hearts by the Spirit. However diverse their personalities or their stations in life, each agree on one very important point: the church of the new millennium has arrived at a major intersection, a Cross-road, if you will, and must return to the biblical revelation.

There are many pastoral obstacles and many

ministerial challenges that must be overcome; and many congregational burdens that must be borne. Because this is so the Bible instructs us to create an ambiance of joy for our pastors and ministers. God has not called us to make ministry a misery. Our contribution is not to make ministry a drudgery but to make it joyous.

Why would anyone want to make things harder for their pastor? But, some do.

But God Is Still Working
Dr. Jonathan Powell

I have been blessed to serve in the ministry of the Gospel of Jesus Christ since 1990. It was then, during a Vacation Bible School service, while playing the piano that I surrendered to God's call to ministry. At that time I sensed a strong call to music ministry.

For fifteen years, I labored and served churches as a Worship Pastor. I enjoyed the music ministry immensely; and, I enjoyed serving God through the music ministry. Church was a "haven of rest" for me. During that time, however, and during the years that followed, I was fighting an inner battle against an unknown enemy, and enemy that was working within me. Years later the source of this inward battle was identified -- a diagnosis and a prognosis were developed. Here's a brief exposition of my story, for His glory!

Since 1995, I had been in a Spiritual struggle. The enemy? Depression. I had very little awareness of depression, its causes or its cure. As a Southern Baptist from Alabama, depression was an ugly word. People whispered about depression but seldom did they talk openly about it. A Christian shouldn't entertain notions of having depression.

However... As a student at the University of Alabama in Tuscaloosa, I was fifteen hours away from graduating as a high school band director when I was told that "I wasn't a good enough musician to make it." That was a big blow, especially after spending four years at the school.

However... God had a plan through it all.

In the winter of 1996, I transferred to Jacksonville State University and finished my music education degree. I became a high school/middle school band director. During this time period, I also helped coach Girls Basketball at my home high school. It was there that I met my beautiful and supportive wife, Jeniffer.

I took my first job at a school in 1997. I enjoyed all of the success in the world that a person could've imagined. During this job, Jeniffer and I were married. The year was 1998. What an amazing wedding, what an amazing marriage and what an amazing woman. When we spoke the vows, "through sickness and health" and "from death do us part", little did we know what the future had in store for us.

I taught school for ten years, serving three schools. The first two schools, I stayed for four years and the last for two years. Thankfully, I never "lost" a job and I always left on my own terms. Success was the norm for my programs. The bands were always successful and superior. Of course, some years were better than others, but each year had its share of bright moments.

I had a principal in my first school that gave me

some advice that I've thought about often, especially over the past few months. He said "Jon, when you're on a high, you're on a high. When you're on a low, you're on a low. You need to find a happy medium."

Little did I know how right that "ole football coach" was. Now the story begins.

On August 26, 2000, after a sleepless night and running from the call to preach for two and a half years, I surrendered to that call. I'll never forget waking my wife up at six in the morning. We cried together, then called the entire family, our pastor, and just celebrated. However, we both knew at the same time that our lives were about to change radically.

The following December I was ordained and accepted the position of Associate Pastor/Worship Pastor at the church where I was already serving. Unfortunately, that church had a rough history of fussing, fighting, and splitting. Our time there, however, was a time of blessing. The people adopted us as their grandkids. The choir was second to none in the area. It was a tremendous blessing. Then 2005! A church contacted us about being their pastor!

The church had experienced tremendous growth under their previous pastor. He left to serve as pastor of a larger church in a larger community. He left behind a great youth program and a really fine congregation. God literally led Jen and I to this church to be their bi-vocational pastor. I accepted the church in August, 2005. I had a heart attack, my first heart attack, the week before my first Sunday!

Talk about an eye-opener. In the two years at this church, I had the privilege of seeing thirty-eight souls accept Christ as their Savior. It was an awesome first church. It was the place where our first daughter was dedicated. It was the place where we first experienced the kindness of a church toward their pastor and family. To this day, that particular church treated us the best, with honor, dignity and respect.

In August 2007, I sensed the call to go full time in the ministry, leave public education, and move forward. That's when the drama began.

My first "full-time" church was in a small community. The church had experienced its glory days in the early to mid 70's, but had declined, with an average attendance of sixty-five per Sunday. I truthfully had doubts of "how can this place grow" and "are they going to adequately take care of my family?"

God chased away those fears. Here's what God did during our four year ministry at that church. We saw 160 individuals accept Christ, baptized 110, attendance grew from the 65 to as high as 320. It was an amazing experience.

With the Spiritual highs of seeing so many souls saved, as a family, we began experiencing attacks from the enemy. During the time period from 2007-2011, we had 15 surgeries, ranging from minor to major. This was the beginning of our financial difficulties. Our thoughts were this, "We're following God, why this? Why now? Why?"

In the middle of the fourth year, I began to get the "itch" and search for church openings that would "better provide" for my family. Of course with the high baptism numbers, folks responded. One church in rural Alabama and one in a major city in Alabama contacted us. After prayer on my part and not listening to my wife's intuition and discernment, we took the church in urban Alabama.

Before our first Sunday, a major F4 tornado wiped out the entire community surrounding the church. The church escaped major damage, but many parishioners lost their homes and a few lost their lives. Yet through it all, God opened doors of ministry that I could've never imagined. People were being saved, including my own daughter. We had baptized more in a six month period than the church had baptized in years. However, we could never find a home in the city, due to the tornado damage. Thus, we'd drive 132 miles one way three days each week to lead this congregation. On September 23, 2011, our second beautiful girl was born. The church was so gracious to us during this time period. Souls and lives were being changed as I preached through Ephesians, then the unthinkable occurred. On November 15, 2011, I suffered a massive heart attack. I was 37 year old. It was near fatal, as I went into ventricular fibrillation at a local ER. It took them 90 seconds to revive me. Did I see lights or any of the such? No, I did experience peace -- Peace that I will never fully comprehended until I reach the other side. At that point, I couldn't preach again until January. I was constantly struggling with depression. Depression was rampant during this time period. Up to that point in my life, I'd never experienced full blown depression, but wow. It was a tough time for me and tough on my family.

January came. Oh! What a January. We had someone saved every Sunday and baptized someone each week. After meeting with my cardiologist, he determined that it would be best to resign the church, stay in our hometown and start over. Thus, I met with the deacons the following Wednesday night, handed each one a personalized letter, and resigned the following Sunday. It was a painful day, yet guess what, someone got saved! Even in the midst of a trial, God still saved.

As we came back home, I took a church as their Associate Pastor. It was a good experience for one and a half years. It was a time of healing, but financially it was a tremendous struggle. We were not making ends meet. As Pastor Fred Luter would say about his mother, "we were barely making ends wave at one another."

In 2013, a church began to call and continued to call over and over. I continually said no. I declined the church's invitation three times. On the fourth time, they were persistent, and I met with their committee. I presented them "guidelines for a pastor" and what I expected out of them. As soon as the church I was serving heard about the meeting, I was asked to quietly resign and say I was taking the other church, before the other church voted. Thankfully the vote was 100% the night I resigned as Associate Pastor.

For the first three years as Senior Pastor at this church in Northeast Alabama, God richly blessed. We focused on prayer, evangelism, and missions. God truly worked. Souls were saved, lives were changed and families were mended. It was a great time. The church experienced rapid growth in all areas. God was working. Looming on the horizon, however, was the darkest time in my life.

Naturally, I am a "doer". If something needed to be done, instead of delegating, I did it. I coordinated our sports ministry, I coordinated this and that. I was burning out at a rapid rate. My preaching was suffering and the church was suffering. Our deacon body, with exception of two good men, were clueless. Then it happened.

On the second Sunday of June in 2016, I preached a sermon about "Division" from Acts. The phone started ringing off of the hook. Accusations were made that I was trying to split the church. In angst, I did tell a young leader in the church to start looking for a place of worship. Furthermore, I completely shut down all levels of communication with all leadership. I was a recluse. It got to a point the Monday following that sermon, I broke. I was questioning my salvation. I was questioning if there even was a God in Heaven above. I was angry at people, I was angry at God, I was a mess. That night, my wife asked me to go to my parents home and plan on going to the doctor the next morning. Before I left, we sat on the edge of the bed, scared to death, not knowing what was next. She agreed for me to stay in another room in the house, then get up and go to the doctor.

That night, I blew up my phone texting a church member who had gone through a similar situation, getting advice from him instead of going to the Lord in prayer. I thought I could solve the problem. Little did I know that I was making the problem worse! The next morning, I went to the doctor and ended up in the local ER. They determined that I needed help, outpatient help, thank goodness. First, with a local Christian counselor who was and is a God-send. Second, with a psychologist. The church, putting on a good face, at this point, gave us a six week sabbatical to get our mind right and put back together. It was a paid sabbatical. The meeting(s) with the counselor helped stabilize my mental and Spiritual state. I kept quoting Psalm 56:3 through the process, "When I am afraid, I will trust in you." The meeting with the psychologist was life altering. She pointed out many things. First, she said there was a reason for the "four year" job change cycle – a manic issue. Second, she stated the depressive issues from the heart issues were a part of manic issues. Third, the "ups and downs" I was experiencing, were manic issues. She diagnosed me as Bipolar 2 or the lower diagnosis of Bipolar Unspecified. Thus, here comes a cocktail of medications.

During the six weeks, unknown to me, the deacons were devising a plan to eliminate me as their pastor, blame my health so they could come out smelling like a rose. Secret meetings were being held throughout the week, some at church, others at member's homes. "Smelling a rat", I declined to meet with them until the first week of August, prior to returning to the church. I had a friend of the family come in from Atlanta to join me as an intercessor partner that night. Lord have mercy, that opened a powder keg.

The meeting was fiery at times. Deacons claiming that many folks had been hurt and that I should've communicate my illness with them. My reply back was how could I communicate my illness with you, especially since I didn't know it was a problem to begin with. Finally, my intercessor spoke up and brought things under control. I had gone into the meeting with a spirit of reconciliation, trying to make things right. Many of the deacons came in with a pharisetical attitude of 'can we eliminate him tonight'. The chairman wasn't even going to pay me. It was a blow. After their consulting period, they allowed me to preach the first Sunday in August.

God moved in that service like you wouldn't have believed. Lives were radically altered. The church body, minus the deacons and their wives, was unified. Immediately after the service, the deacons had a secret meeting and voted me out 6-2. Did they inform me of this that day? NO. They waited until Wednesday night following prayer service. They informed me of their wishes. At that time, I said, "find me a calendar". I mapped out August 28 as the last Sunday. My heart is and was for the church, who was totally caught off-guard by this rash attack. The deacons all thought they were getting off "scott free" in the process. Unfortunately, the church lost many members. Thankfully, no one followed us. Frankly, we didn't want to go to church for a while. Without good friends in the ministry, we'd never have been active again. We were destroyed. Hurt beyond belief. Financially, we were decimated. Emotionally, we were angry. Yet, through it all, God still opened doors.

Pastor friends, sensing the pain, called and asked me to preach. Others, sensing the anguish, took me to lunch and even offered help. It's a blessing when God's people actually are acting like the church. In November, a dear friend asked me to preach for him Sunday and Sunday evening. We fell in love with the church and they fell in love with us. Our kids fell in love with their AWANA ministry. We fit in! In January, we joined the church.

After joining the church, another small church in

rural Alabama asked me to come preach. The services were great. One accepted Christ. The deacons wanted to talk after the evening service. We spoke and left in good spirits. Honestly, Jen and I felt that this was a possibility. Guess what, the deacons spoke with the six deacons from the other church and literally destroyed my character, my family, and that opportunity. Anger appeared again. I've been blessed that God has forgiven me time and time again from anger, frustration, etc. The thing is this, when leaving the previous church, I did my best to reconcile the correct way. It's amazing how we as church people are out to destroy others! To this day, some of the deacons will not speak and if seen at an eating establishment or grocery store, will walk the other way.

How am I today? From broken to being mended. God has used this time of chaos for His glory. Are we broke beyond broke? Yes, barely putting food on the table. Are we still struggling with hurt? Yes, however God is healing the hurts. From the moment on March 22, 1981 when I accepted Christ to this date in 2017, I would've never imagined having two heart attacks, six stents, a diagnosis of Bipolar 2, baptizing 300 new converts, and being run off from a church. But through it all, I realize Romans 8:28 is a literal blessing to all who will read it and take heed to it:

"And we know that all things work together for good to them that love God, to the who are the called according to His purpose" KJV

Why did we go through everything? I'll never know. I do know this however, what Satan meant for harm, God meant for Spiritual growth. Today, I'm serving as a staff chaplain at a local hospice organization and currently following God's lead and call in beginning an evangelistic ministry both preaching and worship leading.

"I don't know about tomorrow, but I know who holds my hand"

Please Understand Me

This pastor appreciation poem speaks of the reasons we need pastors but are too uncomfortable to admit.
We would never tell you this, but we are afraid;
Afraid that our lives will end and few will notice.
We would never tell you this, but we are lonely;
Surrounded by a crowd we're all alone.
We'd never tell you this, but we feel empty;
There's so much more to life but we can't quite reach it.
We would never tell you, but we're disheartened;
No matter how hard we try, a meaningful life escapes us.
We'd never tell you this, but we are worried;
Worried about tomorrow, worried about the past.
We would never tell you, but we're unfulfilled;
Our lives are full, but our hearts aren't satisfied.
We'd never tell you this, but we're searching;
Longing for something to make sense of it all.
We would never tell you, but we need someone to care for us;
Someone who accepts us for who we really are.
We'd never tell you this, pastor, but we need you more than you know.
A Pastor Appreciation Poem by Daniel Sherman http://www.my-pastor.com/pastor-appreciation-poems.html

Deborah Taylor
My Three Crosses

--- Commentary / John Dee Jeffries ---

Art and its many expressions, be it poetry or painting or prophecies or otherwise, are often born of sorrow. Through art we see, not only what the artist saw, but, on a deeper level; we see into the inner person, the artist. Like Christ, many artists are sorrowful, acquainted with grief and suffering. Like the Old Testament prophet Jeremiah, these sorrowful artists weep through their prophecies, poetries and paintings.

These artist often cry the sad cry of abandonment and isolation. With a singular voice, in unison, from different generations, different cultures, they ask one of mankind's most vexing questions: 'In times of trouble why is God a stranger in the land?' They mourn the sad absence of God and together they join Jesus in crying the cry of estrangement: 'My God, My God, why… why…why hast Thou forsaken me?'

The answers, the answers to these vexing questions

are first and foremost, theological, between God and man. Yet, the answers are also sociological, between man and man; and psychological, between a man and himself. And, finally, they are ecological, between man and his world.

Through circumstances beyond her control Deborah Taylor experience deep pain, suffering and sorrow -- and emerged as a new person, a poet for Christ.

My Three Crosses
Deborah Taylor

In 2005, my husband left me for his boss' twenty-year old daughter who was nine months pregnant. Believe it or not, that was good news. I just praised God for the pay increase and for taking out the trash. I knew God heard my prayers and delivered me from "the evil man".

We both had decent jobs and I thought everything was fine. One afternoon as I was driving back to work after lunch, I saw my husband walking down the street, hand in hand with what I thought was a very large young woman. When I got closer, I realized that she was not a large woman, she was a very pregnant young woman. I had to go back to work and finish the rest of my day, in complete shock. It was not easy to finish out the rest of my work day and stay focused. When he came home that night, he knew he was "busted" and he told me that he was getting his things and he was leaving. He told me that he was in love with that girl and wanted a divorce. Then, she came knocking on my door. I saw a red headed woman through my peephole and asked him if that was her. He told me it was. He begged me not to open the door. At the time I was more concerned about his feelings than my own, so I did not open the door. That shows you how ignorant I was at the time. He just grabbed some of his things quickly and left. So, after ten years of marriage, just days before Thanksgiving, I was all alone.

I had just transferred from the one department to another within the county, with a pay increase. Once I got over the shock, I became very angry. I always knew that God was there and I believed that He had my back, but I was crushed. I was all alone and then fear gripped me. I didn't know how I was going to pay all of the bills myself. I didn't know how I was going to make it. I was crushed, but I didn't know devastation, yet. After my husband took some things and left, the electricity was immediately shut off. He had called the utility company and had it shut off in advance. When we got married, the utilities were in his name. It never dawned on me to add my name. When I called them to ask they turn the power back on, they told me they could not because my name was not on the account.

Later that same day, my mother called to check on me. I was so upset and distraught at the time that I could not even speak. I could not stop crying. I went to take a shower and I will never forget what happened next. I was so "torn up" that I can't even explain it, but God knew what I was feeling. While I was in the shower, I heard God say: "Deborah, I love you!" I knew it was God. It was not an audible voice, but trust me, you know when you hear God. HE called me by name! I will never, ever forget that day.

It was very difficult to go to work every day and stay focused, but I did what I had to do and my job was all that I had, I thought. I kept telling myself that everything was going to be alright, as I fought complete hopelessness, utter loneliness, devastating depression, the deepest, darkest despair, humiliation, disappointment and tremendous heartache. I knew what the Bible taught about "renewing our minds" with the Word of God so I tried to stay focused on His Word. I listened to the Calvary Satellite Network (CSN) every waking moment when I was not working. "CSN" is a Christian radio network that features great sermons and wonderful worship music. The sermons and the music helped me so much.

I actually felt like a child that had been left in the woods alone to die. I cannot even explain how excruciatingly painful the feeling of abandonment and betrayal was. I never knew how strong I was until that day, but I know that it was the LORD's strength. I know that HE carried me. I had difficulty sleeping because I was so upset. I lost my appetite and I had no peace at all. I lost so much weight that people didn't recognize me at work. I felt completely unloved, unwanted, unnecessary and hopeless. I felt like my life was over. I was taught that if you commit suicide you would go straight to hell, so the fear of hell and the Grace of God protected my mind from suicidal thoughts.

The spirit of fear gripped me and tormented my soul. I just kept pushing all of those feelings deep down inside of me because I did not know how to deal with them. All I knew to do at that time was cry and pray that God would have pity on me. I learned the hard way that, though God is loving and longsuffering, He is not moved by our tears. He does heal the brokenhearted, but that does not make everything better. He is moved by humility, fervent prayer, faith, seeking His face and true repentance. I did not have a clue how to fight back and I had nothing left to fight with. I took comfort in my faith in God and the fact that God had given me a new job with an increase in pay. It took a while for everything to process before I actually got down on my knees and cried out to God with all of my heart.

I can look back now and see that God was carrying me, because everything was a blur. I had no real friends and no family around to comfort me. I was used to being alone and handling everything myself, I thought. I just continued to go to work and pretend like everything was fine. Even though it was a huge blow, it didn't bring me to my knees in true repentance and full surrender. I was not utterly broken and destroyed, yet. I knew in my heart that God had done me a favor getting him out of my life. I was taught that: "You make your bed, you lie in it." I knew the Bible taught that God hated divorce and I think at that time, I actually believed that getting a divorce would send you to hell. That is not true, of course. I had grown up in church all of my life, but I didn't know anything yet. God was just preparing me for "Boot Camp."

Six weeks after my husband left me, I was in a freak accident. All I remember is waking up in excruciating pain 24/7 and begging God to put me out of my misery. I was in and out of many hospitals and had several surgeries over the next few years. I was admitted to the hospital at least twenty-five times to receive nerve blocks for pain. I heard every bad report you can imagine. I was told that I may never walk, sit or stand again. I was told that I might lose my right arm and hand because they may have to amputate them.

Later, I was diagnosed, among many things, with Regional Sympathetic Dystrophy (RSD). The heart surgeon, who was a Christian, told me to pray that I would ever be able to use my extremities again, if they didn't have to amputate. I had a wrist-jack fixator on my right arm and hand, but my hand was inverted because of the way that I fell. When the surgeon put the nails into my hand, wrist and arms, the nails did not go where they were supposed to. The bone on the outside of my right wrist was too fractured. There was so much nerve damage that I had to wait another year just to have those bones removed. The swelling got so bad that eventually I had to receive the same whirlpool water therapy they give to burn victims. The skin on my fingers, hands, wrist and arm turned black, died and began to peel off. You can look at my right hand and fingers and see they are smaller than my left. My hand and fingers looked like burnt hot dogs on a grill and the skin died, just like when a person is burnt 100%. It was the absolute worst case scenario.

I spent the next few years receiving physical therapy and pain management therapy, without insurance. I saw many specialists, surgeons, physical therapists, doctors and emergency room physicians. Needless to say, I was in excruciating pain for the next few years and all I could do was beg God to take the pain away or take me home. He did neither. For reasons known only to HIM, I had to suffer, but Jesus showed up to go through it all with me. From the first morning I awoke up in the hospital, Jesus sat on the edge of my bed and held my hand. I could not see Him, but I felt His Presence and I knew it was Him. When Jesus shows up, you know it! I was not hallucinating. Jesus was right there with me. I even caught pneumonia on two separate occasions while in the hospital and had to be put on a respirator for weeks each time. I really just wanted to die more than anything else. I felt that there was no reason to live and I was tired of suffering so much.

As I was suffering through all of this trauma, I lost my job, health insurance, vehicle, rental home, everything. But, God had mercy on me and performed many supernatural miracles on my behalf. He used so many angels unawares to help me. He sent strangers to feed me and drive me to doctors, therapists and hospitals. He even put it on the hearts of total strangers, county employees, to donate their sick time, vacation time and personal leave so I would continue to get a paycheck. But, even that only lasted so long.

I found out later that my Boss actually went before the Board of Supervisors to request they hold my position open an extra year, and his request was approved. The County's policy only required they hold a job open for one year when an employee goes out on disability. After two years, it became obvious that I wasn't returning any time soon, if ever. My employer had no choice but to fill my position. I know God will bless everyone involved for their kindness and compassion, especially my former supervisor. I pray daily for all of those who visited me and helped me. God knows their names even if I do not. What you do in secret, He rewards openly.

Next, I was told by my landlord that he had no choice but to rent my unit. He told me that my x-husband had already cleaned everything out. They took all of my personal belongings, everything I owned. I had nowhere to go when I was finally released from the hospital for the first time after the accident. God sent complete strangers to the hospital to take me into their home, care for me and drive me to all of my physical therapy and pain management appointments. To protect their privacy, I will not be giving details but I will forever be giving Glory to God for using these wonderful people to take care of me. I know that he will bless them richly, beyond measure for their compassion and kindness. I will mention that they were not Christians at that time. They were good, decent people with compassionate hearts that God used. God can and will use anyone with a willing heart. GLORY, GLORY TO GOD!

A lot of disappointing things happened during this period. There were many personal tragedies, not the least of which was my father passing away. He had been in a V.A. hospital for years. I was extremely disappointed that I was physically unable to get on a plane and go to his funeral. My father did not recognize me or anybody the last several years of his life. It was a very difficult period. There was much pain and disappointment, but God carried me through it all. Another reason to give Him Glory. It seemed like my life was never going to get better and I just didn't want to be here anymore.

Since I had just received my first disability check, I was finally able to start from scratch, and I mean scratch. I was able to rent an apartment. God supernaturally provided for me. He used strangers to bring me furniture and whatever I needed. I may have lived off of peanut butter without jelly, but He kept me healthy and alive. Thank You JESUS! Glory to God, again!

Finally, after four years, He took the excruciating pain away. I still had pain, but it was not unbearable. I knew He was healing me. I praise God for making me go through the fire, the flood, the pain, the suffering, the torment, the loneliness, the trauma, the heartache, the humiliation, the loss, the lack, the frustration, etc. all by myself. He showed me that HE ALONE is my Healer, Provider, Deliverer, Protector, Mother, Father, Best Friend, Brother, Sister, Husband, Priest, Prophet, King, Judge, my EVERYTHING!

I have three scars in the shapes of crosses on my right forearm, hand and wrist from the wrist-jack fixator. I praise HIM every day for my three crosses. They are a daily reminder who He is, what He has done and what He can do. He is "the same yesterday, today and forever" and if He will do it for me, He will do it for you! Amen! BLESSED BE HIS NAME FOREVER! TO GOD BE THE GLORY, GREAT THINGS HE HAS DONE!

Contact Information
Deborah Taylor

At this writing Deborah Taylor has authored one book...
The Lord Is Our Defense

Order your copy of Deborah's book today
It is available through Amazon,
Barnes and Noble, Books-A-Million,
and wherever fine Christian books are sold.
ALL THINGS ARE POSSIBLE
Deborah Taylor

Broken Beyond Belief -- But Not Beyond Faith

Based on 2 Kings 6.17: And Elisha prayed, and said, LORD, I pray thee, open his eyes, that he may see. And the LORD opened the eyes of the young man; and he saw: and, behold, the mountain was full of horses and chariots of fire round about Elisha. I dedicate this poem to Prophet Brown and his lovely wife, Rebeccah.

Say it, say it, say it, until you see it, see it, see it.
It will manifest if you declare and decree it.
The servant told Elisha: "What shall we do?"
"We are surrounded, they'll kill me and you."

He was full of fear when he saw all the men.
Elisha said: "There's more with us than with them."
He asked God to open his servant's eyes.
The servant looked up in great surprise.

The servant saw many fiery chariots.
God smote the enemy with blindness.
"How big is your God?" Is the question for today.
With faith, all things are possible when you pray.

Let us see Your angels all around.
In the air and on the ground.
If needed, an angel can manifest;
One stood by me while going through a test.

Most are like Thomas, who can only believe:
If they see for themselves; then they're relieved.
If you're in a lion's den or a fiery trial;
You'll see for yourself, there'll be no denial

Terry Martin
The Girl from Phonexville

Some people are seemingly handed everything on a silver platter. Most are not as fortunate. Some, on the negative end of the economic spectrum, start life with little or nothing. They're in a deep hole from the get-go…and a large segment of this portion of the population never climb out. They're the "significantly disadvantaged" -- they're stuck!

It's tough for some people in our materialistic culture to realize that success in life is possible without a rich dad, a large inheritance or a silver platter. On the other hand, there are some wonderful people who have beaten the odds and climbed out of that hole and enjoyed success in life. Many of them started with nothing, and through hard work, talent, grit, and a bit of sweat, managed to rise to "do quite well, thank you."

Many of them even credit their hardship with giving them the motivation, understanding, and personality required to move forward in life. These are the people who inspire us to continue to fight through hard times.

Terry Martin is one such person. Her life

demonstrates just how far determination, confidence, and perseverance can get you in life, even if you start from the very bottom. Terry's life message is clear: it's possible, no matter who you are, no matter where you are, it's possible for you to overcome just about anything, from dysfunctional parents, flawed families, extreme poverty, mental illness and more.

The Girl from Phonexville
Terry Martin

My story begins shortly after the age of four. The only truth I know about my birth is what my mother told me. She said that she asked the nurse to come and take me. (She wanted to throw me across the room).

Mom said she was sick and for some strange reason she was trying to threaten and manipulate dad to do what she wanted, whatever that meant?

I never asked or questioned my mother as to when or where I was taken upon discharge. I didn't know if I was taken to my parent's home or to be with other people.

My mother said she had mental issues. Even so, I know one thing: I always loved my mother. I still love her. I loved her dearly. I could never nor would I ever hurt her, especially by asking so many questions (as a little girl I wanted to know. I wanted to ask those questions).

My father was an alcoholic. It seemed that things were better for us when he was not at home. I say it was best because it was a little more peace-ful when he was not there.

My parents were very destructive to one other. I'm not sure I realized it at the time but it appears that way to me now that I am older. The story about my birth is the only story I ever heard, from childhood to this very day. Surely, by now, now that I am older, I could finally ask about the beginning of my life!

Dad passed away when he was 60 and I never asked him any questions. Now, when the time came to finally ask after all of these years the ques-tions that plagued me, my mother only says, "I don't know," or "I don't remember."

However, I felt that perhaps the pain of talking about the past was too much for her, too much for her to speak about or think about. I think this might be the case because her mind is sharp as a tack.

I tried questioning relatives, but most of them have passed away and no one else knew the an-swers. My siblings were all born in the same hospital, but I was born in Phonexville near Philadelphia. Dad was in the service for a short while and this could account for the different "where" of my birth, but then comes the question concerning the "where" of my birth. "Where?"

Since I can't remember my infancy of course, I can only recall from then until I was 17 yrs old. I lived in at-least 26 different homes that I could remember which included foster care (someone who my father met at a bar, not from a legal welfare placement, and not good might I add), aunts and uncles, grandparents or whomever would help out. Our family was always in constant upheaval and people were always taking us in.

If we were with our parents, it was almost always in poverty-stricken places or until the landlords chased us out from not paying the rent.

I have nothing from my childhood. All I have is a little saying to describe my childhood, a little saying that I came up with one day: "I learned the best bad examples of what not to do or be." For this I am most grateful – I learned!

My husband took me to the location of the hospital where I was born. It's now a college.

For some reason, I'm not sure why, it seems that we all have innate feelings and desires to see where we were brought into this world and to hear those fun stories about how excited and happy our parents were when we were born.

However, upon leaving the exit after visiting my birth place , my feelings were…I wonder what my parents felt like taking their new little girl home? The one new child they were not capable of caring for, and they already had one daughter before me. Now I wonder who else kept me for a period of time, as it seems pretty impossible that my mother could have kept me. Throughout the years when some of the other children were born, I saw other people taking care of them, and now I realize, it more than likely that it was the same for me.

I must say here, my parents are forgiven, for no matter what they chose I still loved them anyway. I believe that love is built inside all human beings and that no matter what parents do there is that connection that can't be severed even if the situation is bad.

Somehow, I believe myself and my siblings have

always sheltered our parents from any hurt, and our parents didn't see or hear the life their children lived. We were so desperate for love that we overly gave everything little children could possibly give. We each tried to make up for the lack of a normal family life while growing up by some of the examples I will speak of in the coming paragraphs. Yes, the opposite roles happened where the children became parents and the parents became children.

The stories I write about will not necessarily be in the order of which they happened, but as they come to my mind. When I look back I try to see when there was a fun time to speak or write about and I am finding it almost impossible. The struggle has left me nothing to write but the truth of what it really was like, so my new saying is, "SAY IT HOW IT IS."

One of my first memories happened when I was maybe 4-5. My mother went to visit friends with my sister and I. It was a run down house so very hot and not taken care of. It needed painting inside and out and cleaning might I add, just pure ugly, maybe better said… depressing! The mother that my mom visited had a few children. She also had red colored scragly hair and scabs on her arms and legs, plus she was missing teeth. There was a young teenager guy there who was jostling me up and down on his knees, as my mother was plan-ning to leave us there. He obviously was trying to take my attention away from my mother. My question is simple: how could anyone walk away for any reason leaving their children in such a decrepit place, under barely any watch care by these people who clearly didn't take care of themselves, their house or their children.

The young guy was helping my mother make her escape. He gave me a beautiful bride doll in a box, a gift from my mother. I guess it was a goodbye gift because once again she was going to a hospital for her nerves.

That is all I remember about that time, but as a little girl I knew what it meant. And we were alone with who knows who again…I do remember crying for her. I remember looking at the door and asking "Where is my mommy?"

Years later, I learned that the guy bouncing me was the town weirdo. I also heard that he loved the Lord and was a good person.

Many people think children don't remember such things and get over it quick but I can tell you, they don't.

There would be so many times our parents split up and went back together. Each new time mom would get out of the hospital we felt so fortunate, but it would only be a short time and it would end again. One time we had to go to court and two of us girls had to say who we wanted to live with. I didn't say my parents because I was to young to not tell a lie to stay home with them. I wanted to live with my Aunt Joyce & Uncle Al because they were so good to me. Being so young I had no idea what the court questioning really meant but it granted me to live with them for a while. I do re-member the welfare paying them money for me to be there and going to get a warm furry winter coat that I loved.

Not long after that I was in elementary school living with Johnny and Winnie. These were the people my father picked up at the bar to take care of us. However, many times they didn't get their money that was promised to them. They would feed us mixed potatoes, tomatoes and Marconi often and when I went to bed I could smell and hear them eating good food.

The bed in the summer had no sheets, but the old stripped mattress, a light bulb hanging down from the ceiling and hardwood floor you got splinters from. I must add, no fans. The nights were so long and lonely only to get up to walk to school and be picked on for being so poor and dressed awful.

I remember the first day of school my father didn't bring money for school clothes and I wore an ugly checkered skirt made out of a curtain and white homely dirty sandals. Walking home from school I would think how bad I didn't want to go back to that house and I would think what would happen I wonder if I just kept walking?

One day I told my Uncle Al how bad I was picked on and he went to the school to talk with the teacher. I wondered why he was there? The teacher afterwards called me to go out in the hall and she told all of the kids my hardships and to not pick on me.

I didn't know until later in life what that was all about and what my Uncle did. If he gave me money I would tape it up in an envelope and get a stamp and send it to my mother. If I was given a stick of gum I saved it for her. She would say how she had no money in the hospital and I felt so bad and maybe even guilty if I chewed the gum.

On a funny note, I have children now and they use to laugh when they found my gum chewed everywhere because I wouldn't throw it out. I saved it! Some things stay with you.

Some things that stay with you are the things you would like to forget, but no matter how hard you try, its memory that has to be managed. Throughout the years growing up I would have to grab knives from my mother's hands as she would threaten suicide.

I myself was actually drug overdosed in third grade. My mother put her pills on the top of a high cubbard so we couldn't reach them but one day she asked me to climb and get her one. I liked them because they were like candy so I was licking them but swallowed a few. Long story short I was going into convulsions and in the hospital and ambulance ride I was being asked if I took any pills? I said no and could have died because I wouldn't admit it. I should have had my stomach pumped or did I? I then remembered nothing! I was afraid to tell the truth.

My father was almost always yelling and if I walked in front of the TV he was watching I would get a combat boot in the butt or pulled up off the floor by my pony tail. How could I admit to him what I did?

My mother didn't like to be left alone and so many days she would get us to stay home from school. In 6th grade I had 24 F's on my report card and prayed to God so much always to please not let me fail. But, I still stayed home because mom would threaten to go to the hospital if she was left alone.

So one day I went to school to come home around the corner on the bus and see an ambulance at my house taking my mom away... she had slit her wrist. I cry now writing this and it was in that house I told God I was mad Jesus was born because I wasn't his mother and I would have wanted to be. I knew I was special for some reason. By the way I did pass the 6th grade!

The stories go on and on but by high school I realized I wasn't stupid, and in fact I was worth something. I decided I loved my family but I wasn't God and I couldn't be always feeling it would be my fault anymore. I ended up graduat-ing, getting married and God blessed me with three sons that I wanted all in a row (like a show I watched, My Three Sons), and then I wanted a girl, and then I wanted her to have a sister and God answered my every wish. I loved each child so much that to look at them could make me cry and get a headache from starring at them so much.

How could I, that poor ragged little girl, have been given so many true little baby dolls to hug and kiss, to dress and feed? And to spoil and boast and brag over again and again? Yes, I am a very proud mother.

The problem now is they grew up too fast and I wanted to be the best mother ever. Unfortunately, my marriage didn't last through the child rearing years and I was on my own. All I can say is I didn't have any good examples to follow, everything was going to be how I would have wanted my life to be.

How fortunate my life was that my children didn't get into drink, drugs , etc. I was a strict mother and we always had family meetings that went something like this when things went wrong, "What did I say that you didn't understand?" Or "What did you say that I didn't understand?"

I had no book on parenting with all of the right answers. I was never a mother before! Or another one in another fashion was "You better be glad to see me when I come home from work and not be glued to the packman." To prove that I was serious I grabbed it and threw it out in the garage on the floor because that is exactly what happened when I came home one night!

In other words I had to mean what I say, and say what I mean! Respect and love that I see between my children to this day is so sweet it can be painful. Each child would drop everything for each other and they continually show love beyond measure to each other, to me and to their dad.

Each child has become highly successful, loves God (the biggest stress reliever for me), and have blessed me with six beautiful grandchildren. I am now married to a wonderful man (my best friend) who pushes and pulls me when I say, "What do you think I should do about this or that?"

Twenty-three years ago I invented a para-medical makeup line for accident and burn survivors and a skin care line, on the side while working other jobs for the financial security to raise my family. I vowed to never be on welfare, food stamps or shop at used clothes stores for my children. They would never get free lunch tickets like I had to either!

God has given me many valleys, hills, and mountains so my stories are a life worth sharing to help others because of my experiences. He showed me that the sky is truly the limit!

I have also owned my own newspaper, had my own radio talk show and became a motivational speaker. The one shocker is I also have been for-tunate enough to do some lay ministry. Where am I going with this? You guessed it I bet! Wherever God leads "The Girl from Phonexville!"

Julie Gossack
Julie's Cancer Story

I wonder if I am weird, sadistic, or suicidal- but the more I ponder the more I believe You have given me a faith that sees YOU as the prize and not this earth.

Honestly, this faith is a gift that I can hardly comprehend. It puzzles me and I know others are struggling because I think this way… they want me to cling to life on this earth…. and so, Lord, I lay all this before You.

Julie's Cancer Story
Julie Gossack

I am grateful that I was practiced as a kardiologist before I was diagnosed with cancer. The experience of kardiology has given me many opportunities to guard my heart. I think I would be a total wreck if I hadn't already learned kardiology.

It all started on September 11, 2013, (which just happened to be Ray's and my 25th wedding anniversary), there I was minding my own business.... getting started on a new school year (Ray and I are both teachers at Heritage Christian School in Bozeman). I was doing a little running and biking, lifting some weights, cooking and house-cleaning, and gearing up to teach a couple tests groups for the KARDIOLOGY study.

Little did I know there was a raging battle going on inside my body that was about to present itself in a most furious manner.

For the sake of brevity, I ended up in the Emergency Room with severe abdominal pain. Initial tests revealed a large mass in my abdomen and the doctors thought I had ovarian cancer. Over the course of two days, my symptoms presented themselves strangely and the doctors began to explore other diagnoses.

As my condition worsened it was determined that I needed emergency surgery and so I was transported by ambulance to the Billings hospital, which was followed by a 4-hour surgery, a week's hospital stay, and an 11-page pathology report that revealed stage 4 cancer of the appendix. My prognosis was that I would only live a year or two.

Our family was shocked, to say the least. Although we had lost both of Ray's parents to cancer, there is NO cancer on my side of the family! And, not to mention that fact that we hadn't even heard of appendiceal cancer.

We later learned this type of cancer is very rare. Only one in a million people are diagnosed with it. Not only is appendiceal cancer rare, but the cells involved in my body are even more rare, and my pathology as a whole is unique, one specialist called it "weird". Additionally, the cancer traveled outside the abdominal cavity into my lung cavity, which according to the specialists comprises only about 6% of their cases.

We also learned that people with this kind of cancer are often not diagnosed until it reaches advanced stages because this cancer grows asymptomatic; they do not even know they have it. They often die in surgery because the damage to their internal organs is too great by the time it is discovered.

Since I lived to hear my diagnosis I had wrestle through it. When I first started to wrestle through my diagnosis, a dear sweet friend challenged me with a passage of Scripture. Together she and I read Luke 18:40-43, which records the healing of blind Bartimaeus. The story goes like this:

So Jesus stood still and commanded [Bartimaeus] to be brought to Him and when he had come near, Jesus asked him, saying, "What do you want Me to do for you?" And [Bartimaeus] said, "Lord, that I may receive my sight." Then Jesus said to him, "Receive your sight; your faith has saved you." And immediately he received his sight, and followed [Jesus], glorifying God. And all the people, when they saw it, gave praise to God. (emphasis added)

My friend directed my attention to the fact that many times in Jesus' ministry He asked, "What do you want Me to do for you?" She encouraged me to answer this question as if Jesus were asking me personally, "Julie, what do you want Me to do for you?" For a couple weeks I pondered this question and also my answer.

After much pondering I finally wrote the answer in

my journal. And so, I read to you some excerpts from that journal, with added remarks for clarification. The thoughts I wrote were not intended to be shared publicly, but were only intended to be between me and the Lord; they are my personal and intimate interaction with Him. You may not agree with my thoughts, but it is how I have answered the question before my God in light of my circumstances.

Lord, I am reminded of Job 2:4 where Satan approached You with the proposal to touch Job's body with illness. Satan commented on typical human nature when he said to You: "Skin for skin! Yes, all that a man has he will give for his life."

But Lord, I do not feel this way. I am not willing to give all that I have for my life. My thinking is more like the Apostle Paul when certain trials awaited him in Jerusalem. After being warned in "every city" that chains and tribulations awaited him, Paul responded with this:

But none of these things move me; nor do I count my life dear to myself, so that I may finish my race with joy, and the ministry which I received from the Lord Jesus, to testify to the gospel of the grace of God. (Acts 20:24)

And so I answer the question: "What do you want Me to do for you?" I do not beg for my life, for days, for years. Christ is my life. My life is hidden with Him. I am His and He is mine. I do not chase days of earthly life; rather I chase the Giver of eternal life.

As I ponder my diagnosis and prognosis I cannot muster within me the typical human attitude that Satan told God- "all that a man has he will give for his life." I wonder if I am weird, sadistic, or suicidal- but the more I ponder the more I believe You have given me a faith that sees YOU as the prize and not this earth. Honestly, this faith is a gift that I can hardly comprehend. It puzzles me and I know others are struggling because I think this way... they want me to cling to life on this earth.... and so, Lord, I lay all this before You.

Lord, if you would so desire to heal me from cancer I would gladly welcome that kind gift... and I believe that people would respond just as they did when blind Bartimaeus received his sight- they would give praise to You... my dear husband and my sons; they would praise You and so would I. It would bring You glory and show Your great power and Your mercy... and so, if You choose to heal me, may I walk in a way that would glorify Your great name.

Yet, Lord, I do not beg for that as though imposing a demand upon a God who is already so very merciful. I do not demand of You what may not be in Your sovereign plans. I accept, Lord, whatever You choose to do with my ransomed life; it is Yours.

And so, what is it that I want You to do for me? How do I answer the question that You asked so very many times while on this earth?

Lord, this is my answer; it is the same as that of the Apostle Paul: 1) That I may finish my race with joy, and 2) that I may finish the ministry to testify to the gospel of the grace of God.

More specifically, Lord, I want to finish well. I want to walk in Your joy, joy, joy through this trial. Also, I want to serve others using the gifts You have given me- being a good steward of the manifold grace of God. I ask that You would enable me to complete some of the writing projects that I have started but are yet unfinished, that I may leave these for the edification of the Body. (I will mention that the KARDIOLOGY 101 study and the tools, were the prominent projects on the list)

But this request, too, I lay at Your throne. You may not have planned for me to finish these writing projects. I accept this very real possibility from Your loving hand, just as I accept whether or not you choose to heal me as from Your loving hand. Amen.

How kind of Him to not only allow me to finish the study, but He has also granted me days of life and the breath to prepare and present seminars. How wonderfully kind of Him!!

Now, let me tell you more about the cancer part…. since this cancer is so rare we consulted with specialists in Spokane, Washington and also MD Anderson Cancer Center in Houston, Texas, in an attempt to wrap our minds around it and learn of our treatment options.

There are two treatments for this type of cancer. One is systemic chemotherapy and the second is an intensive high-risk surgery called HIPEC, which includes removing all visible cancer and some organs as well as a 90-minute heated chemotherapy wash applied directly to the internal abdomen.

The effectiveness of the HIPEC is still in the early stages of research and it is still being debated. It is considered the most intense and traumatic of all cancer surgeries because it involves all the body's organs and causes 3rd degree burns to these organs.

(You can google HIPEC, if you like; from a scientific point of view the procedure is rather fascinating. Some people thought the doctor who invented it was crazy.)

Anyway, because of the aggressive nature of some of my cancer cells, the specialists at MD Anderson recommended that I begin treatment with systemic chemotherapy that I could do in Bozeman. At that time, I had only three chemo treatments due to very low blood counts and two bouts with a collapsed right lung. Thus, chemotherapy was suspended and I had the HIPEC surgery in Houston in March of 2014—just over 3 years ago.

We were grateful that the HIPEC was successful and I was able to go for about 2 ½ years before needing to be in treatment again, due to reoccurrence. So, last fall I completed 6 rounds of chemotherapy (with no collapsed lung this time!) and then returned to Houston just 4 months ago for second HIPEC surgery.

Through all these surgeries I am down about 7 organs or so…. and I am missing some parts and pieces of others… (its is amazing what you live without when down size a little… ha ha!)

I had the ultimate "tummy tuck" in this last HIPEC as the doctors didn't have enough tissue to sew me back together. So, they cut some muscles on my left side to gain about 5 centimeters, which was enough to stitch me closed.

I have often joked that I hope the Lord doesn't ask me to do something really hard because I just don't have the guts to do it! ☐

No, really, though, I again have to say that I am extremely thankful that I was practiced at heart-keeping before the onset of this great trial. I think my situation would have been much more difficult if I were still clueless about the doctrine of the heart and how to diligently guard it from sin. Indeed, my difficult circumstances have provided many opportunities to guard my heart from sin.

I've had opportunities to guard my heart from ANGER and PRIDE that says I don't like what I am getting and I deserve better than this—like going through chemo and watching my body age and deteriorate before my eyes. Confessing ANGER and PRIDE as sin has allowed the Spirit to produce in me HUMILTY and MEEKNESS to accept and even embrace God's wise and sovereign plans for my life.

I've had opportunities to guard my heart from DESPAIR and SELFISHNESS that cause hopelessness and an intense self focus—like when I think about the fact that my life will likely be shorter than the average, that I have less time to spend with my family, and that I may not know my future grandchildren. Confessing DESPAIR and SELFISHNESS as sin has allowed the Spirit to produce in me THANKFULNESS and a FAITH that is assured of God's goodness and love for me and my family, that He has our best interest in mind.

I've had opportunities to guard my heart from FEAR and ANXIETY that can paralyze and even distort reality—like when my lung kept collapsing and wouldn't re-inflate—the doctors didn't know what to do with me, and also waiting for the results of my CT scans. Confessing FEAR and ANXIETY as sin has allowed the Spirit to produce in me PEACE and JOY that permeates my heart and breathes the comfort of our God—the God of all comforts.

By far, my biggest battle was after HIPEC #2 in December. Although the surgery was successful since the doctor's were able to remove all visible cancer and also run the chemotherapy profusion, it is no exaggeration to say that I arrived home from Houston broken and fragile on every level—physically, mentally, emotionally, and spiritually. I've experienced some hard things throughout these last 3 ½ years battling cancer, but the pain and trauma I experienced in December was by far the worst in my entire lifetime. Upon arriving home I couldn't even talk about it without crying.

I will spare you all the details, but in summary, I woke from surgery with the epidural pain block not functioning. An epidural is a needle in your back that blocks pain. The fact that this source of pain control didn't work meant that I felt the whole brunt of the HIPEC surgery pain--full on and intense. I could barely get words out of my mouth to tell the nurses, but the instant I did, my room was flooded with medical personnel as they attempted to relieve my pain. In the end, a new epidural was painfully inserted and it took about 24 hours for it to cover the excruciating pain.

The next 5-6 days went pretty well, but towards the end of my hospital stay, the attempt to transition me from epidural pain coverage to oral pain medication was extremely difficult. Again, I will spare the details, but I will say that you couldn't write the script for the series of unfortunate events that went into my suffering 36-48 hours of uncontrolled pain.

These painful and traumatic events were book-ends for my 11-day hospital stay, and when I was discharged and arrived at the home where we stay in Houston I sat down on the bed and just sobbed. I finally felt safe and was thankful that those times of intense physical suffering had ended But, I also knew that the trauma I had suffered was going to be difficult to work through and that I was likely suffering from (PTSD) Post Traumatic Stress Disorder... even thought I didn't really know what PTSD was at the time.

Even before arriving back in Bozeman, I contacted a friend and asked her to help counsel me through this situation. I also obtained some resources on PTSD from the Resource Center that our counseling pastor recommended. My heart was a wreck and I needed to get on it right away and keep on it until it was resolved.

This situation was of utmost priority and I knew I could not let any time pass without working through these issues—for out of our hearts we live (Proverbs 4:23). And so, my first 8-9 weeks recovering from surgery were spent in diligent study, prayer, reflection, discussion, etc., in an attempt to process what happened in Houston and to see it from God's perspective.

One of the things I learned is that when people experience trauma, like I did, they go into a self-protection mode. Protection from whatever may harm them—noises, lights, activity, motion, further pain and suffering, people—and that becomes the driving force of every day. This focus—which is completely normal and totally understandable—is a shift from our created purpose, which is to glorify God (Isaiah 43:7).

And, I saw this shift in my own heart. This kind of self-protection is not walking by faith in God's person and character. Rather, it takes an experience of the past and filters all of life through it. The future becomes guided by this traumatic event and the suffering experienced from the event is imposed upon the future.

Now, sure, self-protection is very natural. In fact, God created us to self-protect. He put inside of us a "fight or flight" response—which is good because it helps preserve the human race! But as a new-hearted image-bearer I am not called to a natural response.

Since I now knew the level of pain that could be experienced, I became extremely fearful and anxious of future pain that I might suffering as a cancer patient—after all I am still dealing with a terminal diagnosis as the doctors fully expect the cancer to surface again. Research shows that I have a 5% chance of being alive at the 5 year mark from my diagnosis.

As so thinking about future suffering, in my own pride and selfishness I thought I didn't deserve such suffering.

My fear, anxiety, pride, and selfishness is an offense against God's attributes of sovereignty, omniscience, and goodness. It says that He is not the Good Shepherd who cares for His sheep and it accuses Him of not being Yahweh Jireh—the God who Provides for all of our needs.

I am grateful for God's Word and His Spirit, for the KARDIOLOGY tools to help diagnose my sin, the gift of faith, and for the help of other people who love Him. God has used these to restore my broken spirit, to comfort my sorrow, to reveal my sin, and to impart—once again—His joy and His peace... all for His glory!

I have a check-up in Houston in a couple weeks and will find out more about what our future holds at that time... more opportunities for heart-keeping, right?

Mary J. Wagner
Burned Beyond Belief

I could hardly wait to see my siblings. My sister was first to come out to the car, the smile was replaced by horror, even my brothers and Mom couldn't stand to look at me. All the mirrors had been removed from the house, then I remembered Moms on the back of her bedroom door. As I walked around the door, a monster stared back at me. It had no ears, just rumpled looking things protruding form the sides of its head. It had no lips, just a crooked slit where lips should be. The nose was gone and replaced by two holes. It had no hair, just stubbles protruding in sparse areas around its head. The terrifying thing that looked back at me was red and looked like raw meat. I must have been holding my breath because it seemed like an eternity until I could catch my breath. I screamed and hit the floor trying to get away from the terrible sight. No wonder my family couldn't look at me, I couldn't either.

Burned Beyond Belief
Mary J. Wagner

Life brings us many ups and downs. God has not given us the ability to lookinto the future which is good, I think. There are many things I would rather not remember about my life, but the truth is, God has used them to bring me where I am today and doing what He has called me to do.

We were sent to foster homes because Mom had a grand mall seizure and was in a coma for over a year. One of those foster homes was one everyone wishes it didn't exist, but does. My grandparents have always been blessings in my life and took Mom and four small children to care for as Mom recovered.

Grandma even swallowed a fly by mistake in an attempt to make us laugh as she read a story.

This is a true story of my first elevator ride in 1962 when I was eight years old and the place was St. Mary's Hospital in Quincy, Illinois. I had been rushed there with third degree burns from my waist up truly I was "On Fire For God".

Our family had reunited after Mom's recovery from her grand mall seizure and it was ironing day. We had a cast iron stove which we heated, and did ur cooking. I told Mom I could stoke the fire for her, but I was so small.

I climbed on a chair to throw the wood in because I was not tall enough to reach it from the floor. I lifted the small can and poured some fuel in the stove, set the can back down on the floor and climbed up on the chair to see if there was any change. Suddenly, a back draft knocks me off the chair and I am on fire from the waist up. I was engulfed in flames and screaming that the house was on fire! As I ran out the kitchen door my sister knocked me down and threw a rug on me trying to put out the fire. Later I learned her hands were burned as she desperately tried to snuff out the fire that was quickly consuming me.

I don't remember much about the next few minutes or the trip to the ospital. Dad was working so Mom sent my older brother across the fields to get our neighbor to drive us to the hospital. My shaking became so intense as they rolled the gurney into the elevator, I fell off the gurney and when I hit the floor of the elevator, my life stopped. In an instant, I was in heaven!

The angelic music was like music that sunk into my very existence. I felt I was filled with the music right down to my very core. A brilliant light engulfed me, it was shining right through me and filling every ounce of my being. The light was so bright I kept blinking until I realized the lights did not hurt my eyes. I was no longer in any kind of pain or burned. As I looked at myself I realize that I was absolutely perfect, not like the flaws earthly bodies have. A peace washed over me like I was in a gentle soaking rain.

I realized I was sitting down. The brightness was like being in a light bulb. I stood up and walked around feeling like I didn't weigh anything. I had a club leg when I was born, but my leg was not bent or shorter and I didn't feel any discomfort of any kind for the first time in my life.

People ask me if I saw anyone I knew there in heaven. No, I didn't see anyone, but I could hear beautiful music that seems to come from everywhere.

I found I was surrounded by singing angels. I could hear the voice of Jesus comforting me. His voice was melodious, like the sound of water in a stream, flowing softly and comforting as He talked to me.

I heard my Dad and he was weeping a prayer to God. "God, if you really do exist, please don't take my baby girl." I sailed down through the clouds to the hospital room where my Dad knelt next to the bed and my lifeless body was wrapped like a mummy. I was suspended at the top of the room, just observing Dad praying. You couldn't see that it was me for all the wraps, but I knew.

I zipped back into the brilliant light and I said, " That's my Dad. you see he does believe in you Lord! Maybe I'll go back for a while?" I heard His response very clearly, "So be it."

Next thing I remember I was back in my body. Time seemed to have no meaning when I returned to my body. When I did semi-wake, I felt pain every where. On occasions I could hear my Dad's voice talking to me. I wove in and out of consciousness. I had small openings for my eyes, nose and mouth.

Every breath I took reeked of burned flesh, a smell no one could forget, especially when you breathe it in with every breath you take.

Questions came to my mind, would I ever leave the hospital? On Easter, a woman who lived in the hospital came to my room, apparently she was the one who donated the funds for the burn center. She looked old to me as she waved from her wheelchair in the doorway. A gift was placed on the table in front of me. The nurses asked if they could open it for me and I blinked my eyes once for yes. They opened the package and there was a Carmel colored glass poodle. I remember thinking, she must think I'm going to make it or she wouldn't have given me a gift.

Most of my days were spent sleeping, guess it was

God's way of helping me through this unbearable time. Questions kept coming into my mind, but I couldn't ask so they replayed over and over every day. Finally the day ame for the doctors to remove my wraps. Dad showed up and my voice wasn't the only thing that didn't work quite right. My arms looked like hamburger.

I couldn't feel with my hands, I could only felt pressure, like they didn't belong to me. The doctors explained because my sensory nerves weren't working so I couldn't feel like I used to. How am I going to use my hands when I can't feel anything?

My face felt like I had a mask on. I saw them take the wraps off, but it didn't feel like it. The only thing I had to see myself with was a serving tray that was so cratched up all I could see was the shape of my head. Why were they trying so hard to keep me from seeing what I looked like?

I could hardly wait to see my siblings. My sister was first to come out to the car, the smile was replaced by horror, even my brothers and Mom couldn't stand to look at me. All the mirrors had been removed from the house, then. I remembered Moms on the back of her bedroom door. As I walked around the door, a monster stared back at me. It had no ears, just rumpled looking things protruding form the sides of its head. It had no lips, just a crooked slit where lips should be. The nose was gone and replaced by two holes. It had no hair, just stubbles protruding in sparse areas around its head. The terrifying thing that looked back at me was red and looked like raw meat. I must have been holding my breath because it seemed like an eternity until I could catch my breath. I screamed and hit the floor trying to get away from the terrible sight. No wonder my family couldn't look at me, I couldn't either.

"Lord," I cried, "if I had known I would be like this I would never have asked to come back." We have heard the saying, "Time heals all wounds." Well if you have aged at all, you know time seems to stand still while you are waiting for this "healing" they talk about. Time did pass but it was over a year before I could go in public.

I learned young that looks are only skin deep. A person may look good on the outside, but their actions show whether they are good on the inside. It is painful when others do and speak harsh things to us. No matter what we look like on the outside, we all bleed the same and cry the same. We may have different skin colors and come from different countries but we are all made in God's image.

Recovery

My siblings would go to school and I started asking Mom if I could go down to the creek. Trees whistled a sad song but still it comforted my soul. I longed to smell the grass but all I could smell was the stench where it had burned down to my lungs. I did notice I could hear pretty well, but as yet today I can't tell which direction sound comes from. I would throw pebbles in the water because my reflection was still more than I could bear, it was like the Twilight Zone or a bad dream.

How I longed to be back in heaven and would cry out to the Lord until I was weeping uncontrollable.

"Lord, why have You left here? Please Jesus, don't leave me here! I don't want to be here with no face! Even my sister can't stand to look at me!"

One day like a ritual, my prayer was the same. The clouds opened up and a light from heaven landed on me. It was all around me, like a warm ray of sun that shone just on me. I felt the presence of someone near and turned around, two angels were standing in the circle flight from heaven. One angel spoke, "Don't cry that prayer anymore."

The other angels said, "We've heard you crying , collected your tears and brought them before the Lord! He said to tell you, "Do not pray that any more, you will not always be this way. God will use it for His glory."

I don't think I said anything, I knew they were telling me the truth. The angels disappeared and I never threw another pebble in the water to break up my horrid reflection. God had heard my cries and in His great love and mercy, sent me heavenly angels to tell me that someday I would be healed.

Between fifth and sixth grade I was healed enough people were talking to me, but I found I had nothing to say to them. I had walls up so high to prevent myself from hurt that I was blunt with everyone hoping they would just leave me alone. The horrid smell of burned flesh had finally left me. I found great peace and joy with the horses Dad trained.

The mirror was like someone mocking me as I tried to keep my promise I had made to a doctor who said I would be able to smile if I kept practicing by fall. My jaws could go up and down like a nutcracker but that was the extent of it. My nerves were being rebuilt and everything created me pain when it touched me. My siblings who finally made me laugh, helped express how they thought I should smile and by the fall I could smile a crooked one. I only had a dimple on one cheek. but it was a smile nonetheless.

At fifteen I was married to a young man who just came home from the Vietnam War and had severe issues that didn't make it a safe zone to live in. At eighteen I was divorced and had two children, the best of the marriage, my wonderful children.

My daughter was a premie baby and was so ill most of her childhood. When she was nine months old the doctors said I had better move to Arizona. I didn't have much in my pocket as I loaded a two year old and a nine month old onto a Greyhound bus bound for Arizona to stay with my sister who had moved there three years earlier, another way placed things in advance.

As I walked down the aisle with the children everyone said the seat was taken, I must have looked a fright but a wonderful black woman offered me a seat next to her and she helped me with the children all the way to Arizona. I didn't know she was an angel sent by God until after the three days on the bus and she disappeared as soon as we reached the terminal.

Life brought struggles as I raised my children but many years later I married the husband I have now, what a blessing. I became so ill and the doctors couldn't find out what the issue was. Once more I was taken back to heaven, forty years later than the first time when I was burned.

Jesus was there to meet me and explained I was born for this season. He explained to me that my real work was now to begin! The rest is a time for another story to share or you can read my book, "On Fire For God".

The Faith Sisters, Inc. is a non-profit Christian organization that I am proud to be the president of. We touch so many lives and one of the outreaches is to help with the children's burn centers. I have written two books and we have five albums out that build peoples faith.

I challenge you to not think of yourself as being so small that God can't use you, thats just silly. If God could use a fly to answer a prayer that my grandma prayed to bring laughter back into four fearful foster children's lives, He can certainly use you. Be encouraged and run the race He has set before

Contact Information
Mary J. Wagner

At this writing Mary has authored

On Fire For God
We Walk Among Angels

Order copies of Mary's books today
They are available through Amazon,
Barnes and Noble, Books-A-Million,
and wherever fine Christian books are sold.

Mary also has 5 albums available
Clippets can be heard on Mary's website:
www.thefaithsisters.com

Anthony Ritthaler
Escaping Depression
Hope, Help and Healing

--- Commentary / John Dee Jeffries ---

Christian author Anthony Ritthaler languished in deep depression. He couldn't explain his depression – it was inexplicable. He couldn't comprehend how such despair could overcome him -- and grip him – it was incomprehensible. And, he couldn't make sense out of the insensible, the insensible complications that afflicted him through his depression. The whole episode dragged on and on and on -- it was irrational, illogical. He could only touch lightly upon his wounds, the wounds of depression as he felt and mourned his loss.

Deep inside Tony knew that Christ and Christ alone was the answer – but the presence of Christ was hidden; then, by God's grace, the Light begin to shine.

Depression nearly claimed my life and I am writing this to give people hope.
-- Anthony Ritthaler

Escaping Depression
Anthony Ritthaler

When I was 20 years old, I went through a deep depression that lasted for 20 months and it nearly killed me on several occasions. There are several words I would use to describe this time in my life -- brutal, miserable, and lonely. Nothing I did would help, and every day was an absolute struggle. Many thoughts of suicide raced through my mind, and every waking moment I felt trapped in the prison of my thoughts. My joy left me, and my desire to depart was greater than my desire to stay. Every single day I would cry so hard that my strength would leave me and I could barely stand. All throughout the day the Devil would replay the same doubts and questions in my mind and it got to the point of me nearly giving up all hope. I felt hopeless, alone, defeated, and my peace and ability to think properly was completely gone. All I wanted to do was sleep and being in depression took more energy from me than playing basketball for 8 hours would. People thought I was crazy, and I started to as well.

During this time in my life I lost my zest for life and I hated to go out in public. There were no friends to comfort me, no song in my heart, and the Devil confused my mind and stole so much from me. Often I would break out in cold sweats and collapse to the ground. It felt like I was carrying a thousand pound weight around my neck at all times, and to be alone was my greatest desire. Often I would look out the window and watch the world race by and tears would fill my eyes because I had no intentions to join them. In days gone by sports were my haven and they were always something that made me happy but during these dark times of my life sports did not help. When I went to church I would watch others shout and all I wanted to do was to go home so I could be alone in my thoughts. My life was filled with shame, confusion, sadness, and misery, and nothing seemed to comfort me. Days felt like nights, and nights never ended. I was defeated, heart broken, weak, fragile, and needy in every way. For a long time I felt like I was destined for disaster and I had no answers. My will to live was almost gone and I almost gave up on life. On the inside I felt like a ticking time bomb, and on the outside I looked like death warmed over.

All throughout these 20 months of depression I pushed myself to God's house despite how I felt and that eventually was the key to getting out of my dungeon of depression. When I was going through this war of depression I refused to go to drugs for quick fixes because I was taught that if I trusted God, He could set me on a solid rock, so I held on with all I had. When hope seemed all gone, help was on the way and in a revival meeting at my lowest point God sent a spirit-filled preacher that was instrumental in getting me out of depression. As he preached that night I felt a power sweep over me that hadn't been there in so long and I hung on every word he said. The spirit of God got a hold of me that night and tears of misery turned into tears of joy as I felt the chains of depression breaking one at a time. My energy returned, and so did my joy and I went to the altar and asked God to use me and take away the dark cloud that hung over me. God answered this prayer from my heart and shortly after that night I started investing in the ministry of God every day of my life. God renewed my mind, healed my heart, and dumped His blessing bucket all over me. Now by the grace of Almighty God, the Lord has given me a wife, a child, a home, and joy unspeakable and full of glory. Every day is fresh and new and His power is felt on a daily basis.

Jesus is able to break any chain that binds us and my life is living proof. God has allowed me to write 8 books, go on 23 radio shows, and help preachers all over the world. The Lord took this broken vessel and He is forming me into His vessel and He can do the same for you. If you feel like giving up, always remember that Jesus can take your broken pieces and make you into something beautiful. Depression nearly claimed my life and I am writing this book to give people hope. If God can salvage me, He can salvage you too. A great man of God said one time concerning his life, and I quote "Satan had a plan, but God had a greater plan. For over 15 years God has allowed me to walk in victory and joy and I never want to go back to the days of depression again". Without God we are nothing, but through His spirit He has given us everything. Trust me, I know how powerful depression can be and it nearly destroyed my life. I'm thankful every day for God's mercy in my life and I desire for you to gain help through the pages to come. Never give up on hope, and never be afraid to run to Jesus. He can weather any storm that comes our way. Thank you Lord for pulling me out of that horrible pit and I pray you do the same for all who desire to escape its torments.

Thanks be unto God, who giveth us the victory.

Don't allow depression to be the end, allow God to

remove it and give you a fresh start like He did for me.

If you have never gone through the deep dark walls of depression, I praise God for that. But be aware that depression can sneak up like a thief in the night. No one is immune to depression, and it can strike anyone suddenly at any moment and it will not ask for permission to attack you. Once depression settles into your life, it can derail you and destroy you if not handled in a timely manner. Depression is nothing to mess around with and my advice would be to do whatever it takes to avoid it at all costs. If you are in your right mind, guard that because depression can take that from you. Depression literally has the potential of taking everything that you love and cherish and turn it into nothing but ashes. Depression in no way is your friend, and we better treat it as our enemy. Satan will use depression to make you feel sad, lonely, and broken. I've seen people that had it all end up on the streets begging and they were just a shell of their former self – all due to depression. I've seen countless singers, athletes, and artists end up on skid row begging for change all because depression took over their mind. Thousands of preachers who were once on fire for God have left the ministry and don't even attend church today all because of depression.

Depression will make you crazy and like a tornado it will sweep over your soul and leave nothing but destruction in its wake. We must be aware of how dangerous depression can be, and we must understand that it can ruin our lives. Whenever we think it can't happen to us, most likely we will be the very person it attacks next. Please don't take depression into your bosom because it will burn you. Depression will take everything you have and want more so let's do whatever it takes to be in tune with God so it doesn't control our lives.

No matter what storm you find yourself in always remember that it's only temporal and it won't last forever. The great Apostle Paul said this in II Corinthians Ch 4:17 "For our light affliction which is but for a moment, worketh for us a far more exceeding and eternal weight of glory". The Bible says "Life is but a vapor" and the trials we encounter down here will be forever wiped away in glory. If the Devil can get you to focus on the nasty now and now he knows he can blind you to the brighter day that is coming. It's very hard to feel depressed when our mind is dwelling on Heaven, so Satan will come along and distract us through things of earth that will take our focus away from the eternal glory that awaits us. The Bible says "Love not the world, neither the things that are in the world. If any man love the world the love of the Father is not in him. For all that is in the world, the lust of the flesh, and the lust of the eyes, and the pride of life, is not of the Father, but is of the world. And the world passeth away, and the lust thereof: but he that doeth the will of God abideth forever". When we dwell only on the temporal things it is a trap of the Devil and it will lead to depression every time. We must realize that Heaven and earth shall pass away but eternal things will remain forever. When we think about Heaven, depression must leave because the Bible says in Revelation 21:27 "And there shall in no wise enter into it anything that defileth, neither whatsoever worketh abomination, or maketh a lie: but they which are written in the lambs Book of Life". Focus on verses like John Ch

14:1-3 and depression will go away. The Bible says "Let not your heart be troubled: ye believe in God, believe also in me. In my Father's house are many mansions: if it were not so, I would have told you. I go to prepare a place for you. And if I go and prepare a place for you, I will come again. And receive you unto myself; that where I am, there ye may be also".

Child of God, it's difficult to sense any depression when our minds are fixed on the joys that await us there. Revelation 21:4 says "And God shall wipe away all tears for their eyes: and there shall be no more death, neither sorrow, nor crying, neither shall there be any pain: for the former things are passed away". Heaven is a place of eternal bliss, joy, peace, freedom, and delight. In Heaven there will be no sickness, pain, fear, death, or depression. Thank God five seconds after we are in glory the pain we encountered on earth will be nothing ***more than a distant memory. The Bible says "For I recko***n that the sufferings of this present time are not worthy to be compared with the glory, which shall be revealed in us". Nothing we face down here could ever compare to the glory we will enjoy up there. The Bible says "O Death, where is thy sting? O grave, where is thy victory". Always keep your eyes on the ultimate prize and life will have meaning. The Bible says "Hence forth there is laid up for me a crown of righteousness, which the Lord, the Righteous Judge, shall give me at that day; and not to me only, but unto all them that love His appearing". The return of Christ is just over the horizon and if we can focus on that depression will fade in the background of our lives. The Bible says in Titus 2:13 "Looking for that blessed hope, and the glorious appearing of the great God and our Savior Jesus Christ". The scriptures declare in Revelation 22:12 "And behold, I come quickly; and my reward is with me, to give every man according as his work shall be". Will you have crowns to cast at His feet or are you too busy worrying about earthly things?

The Bible says in II Corinthians 5:10 "For we must all appear before the judgment seat of Christ; that every one may receive the things done in his body, according to that he hath done; whether it be good or bad". The Bible says that Christ shall return like a thief in the night. The Word of God says in I Corinthians 15:52 "In a moment, in the twinkling of an eye, Christ will return". Focusing on eternal things will thrust us out of depression and it will light a fire under us to be productive for God. Don't allow your life to be consumed with temporal things, allow God's spirit to remind you of Heavenly things and depression will flee away from you. The Bible says set your affection on things above; and if we will have God's mind depression cannot be part of our daily routine. Don't allow Satan to keep you in the prison of your present, but rather allow your mind to be directed by the Holy Ghost and you will have a brand new outlook on life.

Thank God for the saying "This too shall pass". Trials are but for a moment but Heaven will last throughout the ceaseless ages of eternity. Cheer up child of God and rest in the fact that God has a brighter day ahead for you.

Every time I find myself in a storm of depression I slow down, pace myself, and focus on how good God has been, and how much worse it could be. You do not have to read too deep into history or look too far around to discover that compared to other's situations ours is not that bad after all. Praise God through your depression, and thank Him for all the good things you do have. Psalm 33:5 says "The earth is full of the goodness of the Lord". Focus on your blessings, not your problems and understand that it could be a whole lot worse. There is so much to be thankful for.

The greatest advice I could ever give anyone suffering from depression is to run to the blood of Jesus as fast as you can. Nothing strikes fear in the heart of Satan or his demons more than the blood does. Whenever you feel overwhelmed with guilt, ashamed, defeated, dirty, and filthy, run to the fountain filled with blood and you can be clean from head to toe. I John 1:7 declares "But if we walk in the light, as He is in the light, we have fellowship one with another, and the blood of Jesus Christ His son cleanseth us from all sin". It does not matter what fear has a hold of you, the blood can set you free. It does not matter what you have done or whom you have been, the blood can wash you whiter than snow, and make you whole. The Bible says in Revelation 1:5 "Unto Him that loved us and washed us from our sins in His own blood". The old song says "There is a fountain filled with blood, drawn from Emmanuel's veins, and sinners plunged beneath that flood lose all their guilty stains. If you're depressed, saturate your life with songs about the blood, preaching about the blood, and thoughts about the blood and Satan will run from you and depression will run with him. Colossians 1:14 says "In whom we have redemption through His blood, even the forgiveness of sins". The blood of Jesus can bring forgiveness to any sinner and bring you joy on the inside. Colossians 1:20 says "And having made peace through the blood of His cross, by Him to reconcile all things to Himself: by Him I say, whether they be things in earth or things in Heaven". The blood of Jesus can clean up your mind, cleanse your soul, and brighten your future. The Bible says in I John 1:9 "If we confess our sins, He is faithful and just to forgive us our sins, and to cleanse us from all unrighteous".

If you are tired of feeling depressed and defeated the blood of Jesus is the answer for it can give you a brand new start. I Corinthians Ch 6:9-11 says this "Knew ye not that the unrighteous shall not inherit the Kingdom of God? Be not deceived, neither fornicators, nor idolaters, nor adulterers, nor effeminate, nor abusers of themselves with mankind, nor thieves, nor coveters, nor drunkards, nor revilers, nor extortioners, shall inherit the Kingdom of God. And such were some of you: but ye are washed, but ye are sanctified, but you are justified in the name of the Lord Jesus, and by the spirit of our God". Without the blood we will always be miserable but through the blood we are forgiven, and clean in God's sight. Satan cannot handle the blood and when we make much about the blood Satan will choose someone else to bother. Every time you feel vile and unclean just run to that fountain filled with blood and you will feel like a newborn baby all over again. The blood of Jesus has the power to break any chain that binds you and it will remove depression from your life. There is something within the heart of every human that longs to be clean and the blood of Jesus can cleanse every stain. The third verse of There is a Fountain reads like this "E'er since by faith I saw the stream, thy flowing wounds supply, redeeming love has been my theme, and shall be 'til I die". If we can make these words the theme of our life we can walk in total victory and we can kiss depression goodbye.

Thank God for that fountain filled with blood that causes Satan and his demons to run every time. When you're in trouble just claim the blood and depression will scramble in fear.

Contact Information
Anthony Ritthaler

At this writing Anthony has authored…
Walking On The Water With Jesus (Volume 1 and 2),
Soaring With Eagles (Volume 1 and 2),
Roaring At The Enemy and
A Devil From The Beginning.
Escaping Depression

Order copies of Anthony's books today
They are available through Amazon,
Barnes and Noble, Books-A-Million,
and wherever fine Christian books are sold.

Donna Britt
I Can Dance
Because He Loves Me
Donna Britt's * True Love Story

My life is different than most because at the age of 39 on an icy, winter day in November of 1991, I walked out the back door and fell down the steps. I was paralyzed! The doctors in Palestine, Texas said I would not live through the night—but I did! They said I would be on a respirator for the rest of my life if I lived, but the good Lord proved them wrong. I was ready to praise the Lord no matter what happened!

Several months before I fell, an audible Word came to me from the Lord. "What would you do if you lost everything like Job?" I answered, "I would be just like him." Whatever God does or does not do, I will trust Him. Just like the three Hebrew children in the fire, I know the Lord will take care of me. AMEN!

They took me to the East Texas Medical Center (ETMC) in Tyler, Texas and put me in a neck brace. They had to give me a tracheotomy in my neck to help me breath.

I don't remember very much during that time, except that I wanted to die. Jerry said that I kept telling him, for a long time that I hated him for bringing me back

In my despair, I would ask God to let me die—but as you can see, he did not answer that prayer! He had a plan for my life. I may have been angry with Jerry at first, but when I realized that God had a plan for my life, I was no longer mad at him. The only thing that kept me going during the long hospital stay was The Serenity Prayer that I had learned in a 12-Step Co-dependency program at our church. It helped me put things into perspective.

God really began to bless us by caring for our family. A couple from church took the girls (12 and 14 years old) into their home. They were able to give them a safe and loving atmosphere to help them during this difficult time in their young lives and our family. I am so thankful for their

generosity of time and love. God also sent people from many churches, at different times, to pray and let me know that I still had purpose—and a reason to live. "For I know the plans I have for you, says the Lord, they are plans for good and not for disaster, to give you a future and a hope" (Jeremiah 19:11).

Training for a New Life * January 1992 * From Tyler they sent me to The Institute for Rehabilitation and Research (TIRR) in Houston. It finally began to sink in—I had no use of my arms or legs. I was totally paralyzed! The doctors told us that my spinal cord was narrower than normal, probably from birth. Even a slight blow to my head could have caused paralysis at any time in my life.

They started training me to live my life as a quadriplegic. The hospital also trained my family how to take care of all my medical needs, which were many. Before I left TIRR, they told me I could have a life—just as I was. Now I had a reason to live. My family still needed me. At this time, I had three teenagers at home and that made me want to live. My husband still wanted me to live and be a part of his and my children's lives.

Popped Out * March 1992 * The doctors had said I would never be able to get off the respirator. Then God did something great and mighty! I had told the Lord, "If you don't let me praise you, talk to you, tell others about you, and give You all my praise; please don't let the stones have my praise" (Luke 19:40)!

When I left the rehabilitation hospital, I only needed the trach tube when I was congested, but that was two-three times a day. The Lord had the doctors strengthened my lungs so that I could breathe oxygen on my own. When I got home, I never had to use the tube again. THAT WAS A MIRACLE! Then one day the trach started hurting, and I went to the doctor's office. He looked at it and some how
the tube had "popped out" and I was still able to breathe on my own. The doctor sent me to the hospital, but by the time I got there, the opening in my throat had closed up! They called the doctor at TIRR, who had more experience, and he said to leave the trach out. PRAISE GOD! I was so happy. I have never had pneumonia or the need of a respirator for oxygen since that time.

The Big Dilemma * The CNA's (nurse's aides) came out five days a week until the insurance ran out. There was no way I could stay at home without them with Jerry working and the girls in school. Finally, the day came when it did run out. It was a really big dilemma! So we put it into

God's hands. The only alternative was a nursing home and I really did not want to go there. But God worked that out also.

About the same time, my husband was laid off from his job with the railroad. Then a very unusual thing happened. The railroad Jerry was working for said they were going to put him on furlough. That meant he could stay at home and still be paid a regular salary. He would also be able to keep our insurance and other benefits! This was God's plan for us for the next two and a half years. He and the girls continued to care for me and we were still together as a family.

Time of Moving On * January 1997 * I made a simple prayer to the Lord that we needed a change from the way we were living, as it was getting difficult for all of us. The Lord heard my prayer. The railroad told Jerry that they were relocating him to Kansas in March. One of the benefits of his move was that he would receive a settlement that paid off our trailer home and all the other bills.

Another benefit of the move was that the atmosphere of our home was better without the strife between Jerry and me. The children and I were naturally concerned about being without him, but we knew God would provide everything we needed and He did!

In June, Jerry came home for our youngest daughter, Bridget's, graduation. We had talked about moving to Kansas with him, but as the time got closer, I didn't want to move for many reasons. I just wanted to go to a nursing home in Palestine where my children and church family were. God worked everything out.

Watch Out World * December 2000 * The Palestine newspaper wrote an article about me when I enrolled in the community college. One of my class assignments was to write and present a short autobiography including our plans for the future. The following is some of what I wrote for my speech: "I began to feel like I wanted to get my associate degree in liberal arts.

The nursing home was so nice to me and helped in many ways to make this possible. I started going back to college to become a social worker. I had learned that I am intelligent and can do anything I put my mind to do—with God's help. TRC also helped pay for some of my courses and I thank God for all their help. Without it, I would not have been able to go to school."

I think that I still have much to give to my family, the community and the world. I can and I will make a difference in this life. I have already ministered to many people that I encounter wherever I am. People come up to me all the time and say what an inspiration I am to them."

"When I was in the hospital, I told God that if he could not use me somehow, to take me home with Him to heaven. He left me here and He has used me for His glory! My children still need me to help them with life's problems. They come to borrow money from me at times and the girls ask questions about boys. I still feel like mom, no matter what shape I am in physically. Just because I cannot move my limbs, does not mean that I am not useful."

"My life is very rich and rewarding and I am going to live it to the fullest. I have dreams of one day being a counselor. I have always known that I like to talk and help other people. Women have called me to talk about their problems and I have always listened. I enjoy listening to their problems and trying to help make sense of their lives. Because of this, I think I would make a good counselor. I know that I cannot handle their burdens, but God can."

"I would like to live on my own with a health-care provider. I want to be a vital part of society, working and getting a paycheck instead of living on Social Security. I hate living off the government even though I used to work and pay taxes. I am young enough to still work and provide for myself."

On a New Journey * August 2001 * Nine years after becoming paralyzed, I had graduated from the community college with my Associates Degree. I wanted to help people who were in situations similar to mine. I also wanted them to realize that they can do it and many resources are available if they ask and research the avenues. I was only able to go to college because God worked out all the many details and I had a wonderful support group behind me.

I completed my classes with a 3.7 grade point average. I could not believe it, because during my earlier school years my grades were barely passing. I was now ready to go to Steven F. Austin State University (SFA) in Nacogdoches, Texas. The college was equipped for handicapped students with many accommodations and services available for us. I was on a new journey, seeing if I could make it on my own. I was apprehensive and excited at the same time. My good friend, Tilda, went with me to be my caregiver and helped with my class work.

Eventually, I had to drop out of school because of a dangerous bedsore. Actually, I was not upset, because I had found out what I needed to know. I now knew that I could

not live on my own anymore. There were too many things I couldn't handle alone.

When I returned to Palestine, they moved me into a

different nursing home. At first, I didn't like it because it was in another town. Elkhart is a small town with a population of only 1371, located 11 miles from Palestine where all my family, friends and church were located.

It turned out to be a nice home that allowed the residents to have pets. There were big fish tanks and birdcages in the lobby. There was also a resident dog and cat wandering around, that the residents would pet and feed. "Pet therapy" really does work!

Someone even put up a bird feeder outside my window where I could watch them. For a while, I even had a fish bowl in my room! God worked it out again. They gave me a private room and I was still able to keep my van. God worked out things that were more than anyone could ever think or imagine. He just does it! God has, and I know that He will always take care of me.

Email from Donna's daughter, Bridget * December 16, 2005 * It was a typical Saturday afternoon. My father, sister, and I had gone to Tyler, TX that day to do some shopping. We got a call from the nursing home at 8:30 p.m. that night. They told me that they were sending my mother to the hospital. When we got there, the ER doctor was trying to put in a central line in her chest.

A friend who was working in ER told us, "She is septic, which means the infection has gone into her blood stream and we are giving her the strongest antibiotics that we can. However, because she has had so many urinary tract infections, her body is immune to the antibiotics. She is very sick and the only thing that is going to bring her out of this is prayer."

So we went into the waiting room. As we were in there talking, we heard "Cardio to Trauma 1!" It was Mom!

Praise God we heard this because it stopped them from putting a vent on her. She wanted to die without help. We told him "No!" She was a DNR (do not resuscitate). We wanted to obey her wishes and not put her on a breathing machine. We started calling everyone we knew to pray and come to see her if possible. We went back to the trauma room with some friends and family members, and started singing praise songs to her. Thirteen of us just surrounded her with the sound of praise and worship.

At 2:30 p.m. the next day, she was still alive! Her parents from Houston arrived. When she saw them, she started saying, "Mom, Dad! I love you, Mom! I love you, Dad!" She just kept repeating that over and over again. This continued until 10 p.m. Sunday night. She would stop breathing for a few seconds but you could see her heart beating. Then she would take a deep breath and her eyes would open. She would look around the room and whisper, "Jesus! I love you, Jesus!"

My aunt stayed with her Sunday night. At 2:30 a.m., Mom woke up again and looked around the room, still saying "Jesus!" But this time she looked scared. My aunt asked her if she was seeing Jesus and if He was speaking to her. She said, "Yes! Jesus is standing in the light and telling me to come." My aunt said to her, "Are you ready to go with Him?"

"I don't know," Mom replied. My aunt got her to tell Jesus that she didn't know if she was ready. Mom fell asleep saying, "I don't know if I'm ready to come home." Early Monday morning, she woke up in her "right mind" and began talking normally! The doctors were amazed! Two days later, she was back in the nursing home where she is today and doing just great!

There are no words to describe how much Mom has touched our lives. She also blesses many people in this town. Obviously, she is very much loved and God is not through with her on this earth. Her whole focus is

witnessing for Him, because she knows that tonight could be someone's first night in hell and she would rather suffer than to see that happen to someone that she can touch. What a mighty woman of God we have living among us!

Dancing on Wheels * April 2007 * One time, God made it possible to be able to praise Him in the dance with my whole spirit, soul and body. Our church was having a night of drama, music and dance for Easter. I had not even thought of being involved when the director asked me to be one of the "dancers." My daughter, Bridget, and I were part of an Israeli praise dance done in a circle with me in the center of the other dancers.

The night of the program, we were all nervous. The dance went well with no mistakes. It was all to God's glory because of His grace! He helped me through the dance with as much grace as a wheel chair could manage. My chin and neck muscles controlled the chair as I worshiped the Lord. I was truly "dancing" in my spirit! This was my time of "dancing on wheels."

My Dream and Goal * 2009 * Elkhart, TX * At the age of 56 my dream and goal is to shine with the glory of God, the light of Jesus, and with the power of the Holy Spirit. Whether it is here at the nursing home or wherever else, that God may lead me. I want people to say, "There is something different about her." There have been many victories in my life. I did not die! That was a miracle and truly was an escape from death (Psalm 68:20). I finished an associate degree at TVCC, which I never thought possible.

Over the last 10 years, I have been asked to participate in many of the programs at the nursing homes where I have lived. It is a joy to tell people everything God has done for me. Sometimes I sing a solo or give a devotional about something the Lord recently put on my heart. I love speaking at various churches, prisons and other nursing homes.

I started going to prison with some women at our church. Sky View Prison in Rusk, TX invited our group, Be Fruitful and Multiply, to come and minister to the inmates. I always felt so blessed after visiting with the women inmates. The Lord protected us all the time, on our way going and while we were there. You think of that and it can scare you, but you must always remember that God is with you. I was able to tell the inmates how I survive living in a nursing home and living as a quadriplegic.

I may not be in "lock down," but I am in my own kind of prison. I do not have guards, but I do have people in control of my body. I have to deal with all kinds of personalities, some you enjoy some you put up with and some you just have to pray for them. I told the women how I trusted God to help me though. Without Him, I could not wake up in the morning. He is my very life, breath and strength.

Counseling for Him * 2011 * I am now 59 and enjoying my life. Last year I moved into a brand new, beautiful nursing home in Palestine. I am now closer to my family and friends and able to attend church more often. I was among the first residents to move into the home. I am very thankful that I still have a private room, a computer and my van. The atmosphere here is so peaceful and quiet.

The garden is a courtyard with a big water fountain and many beautiful trees and flowers. My friends decorated my room and put up a bird feeder in the garden outside my window.

You could say I have been involved in full-time nursing home ministry since I moved into one in 1997. There are always new people to meet and needs to be met. My greatest desire now is to minister to those who have made mistakes and their lives are not perfect. I want to reach out to the ones who seem so bad that nothing can be

done about them. The Lord has made it possible for me to learn the scriptures by heart. To be able to do this is amazing to me. God answered my prayer to be a "counselor." I go to work everyday for the Best Boss in the world and He sends all those the Holy Spirit has prepared for me to encourage in some way.

My days are now spent praising God! In my room, I love to listen to praise music and teaching tapes. The staff gets me up and into my motorized chair. Then I make my rounds visiting people. We love to talk, sing and pray. They even love my croaky voice when I sing them one of my favorite songs. I am completely free to love and serve Him all the rest of my days.

Dear Reader * 2013 * There is something I want to tell you. He loves you and has a purpose for your life. God is a good God and He has already blessed us so much. I pray that my life will be an example to many and you will begin to see just how great and loving our God is. He has been my strength and protected me. That is why I love to praise Him so much! That is why—I CAN DANCE Because He Loves Me!

In His Love and Service, Donna

"My life is an example to many,
because you have been my strength and protection.
   That is why I can never stop praising you;
   I declare your glory all day long.
   And now, in my old age, don't set me aside.
   Don't abandon me when my strength is failing"
   (Ps 71:7-9).

Anna K. Schmidt
Looking For the Light

--- Commentary / John Dee Jeffries ---

Someone once said, "Never forget in the darkness what God taught you in the light." Corrie ten Boon said, "There is no pit so deep that God is not there." The Bible says that "the people who sat in the darkness have seen a great light."

Anna Schmid knows all about darkness -- and light. She was overwhelmed by darkness -- looked, looked, and looked -- then finally the Light appeared.

Anna's Story
Anna K. Schmidt

Out of desperation, her dad called the police. A policeman came and he knocked on the door and called out through the door for someone to come out. But, no one did. Scenes like this were not a normal occurrence in our lives. Several months ago, Aimee was a dot your I's and cross your T's kind of person. This kind of behavior from her was so foreign to us. The policeman told us no law was being broken. She was willingly in the house, and didn't want to come out, and there wasn't anything he could legally do about it. This was not the news that I wanted to hear! "You're not serious, right? Make her come out! I wanted to get our daughter out of that house, so she could come home! But, no, we had to leave and wait until morning to hear from her. I felt utterly helpless and hopeless! I also felt like a terrible parent!

"How could this be happening to MY family? This isn't the way it's supposed to be! I feel so scared. Why can't they understand me?! I can't believe my parents LIED to me! How could they do this to me...and my brothers? Why aren't they doing more? Why is this happening? I'm sooo tired of feeling misunderstood. What is my life going to look like now? I'm sooo tired of feeling sad and alone. I'm not sure I even care if I live or die anymore."

These were the thoughts of my heartbroken daughter when she was 14 years old. Too young to have fully formed emotionally to be able to gather up any peace of mind of what has happened. Unable to put into words that the family she's known and trusted has completely changed. Her world, and all of ours, had flipped upside down.

As a parent you want to do ANYTHING in the world to protect, love, and make sure your child never feels anything like this. What do you do when you know your child is broken, and don't know how to help? What do you do as a parent when you're broken too? What do you do when the light at the end of the tunnel begins to fade and you're stumbling in the darkness?

This is the reality of my life and that of my daughter in 1998. As a mother, I had hopes and dreams for Aimee. I encouraged her and was happy to help her be all that she could be in this world. I wanted her to have her own opinions and be alright with sharing them and doing what was right in God's eyes.

She was an obedient child and did as she was told. She was loving, thoughtful, smart and did very well in school, played piano and was an outstanding soccer player.

When she was 8 years old, she was the only girl that played on a boys' soccer team. She learned to be tough and held her own as she played with the boys. As a freshman in high school she played on the Varsity team. It was so enjoyable to watch her on the field. She played with such passion!

Aimee began changing and chose a different road than the one that we had planned for her, and that she had laid out for herself when she was 14. One of her high school teachers called me to tell me that she had noticed her grades were declining. She also told me she had written a paper about marijuana and how it should be legalized. She feared she was smoking pot. Great! Just what I didn't need to hear about my sweet Aimee. I was saddened and surprised by her phone call. I found it odd that a teacher would take the time to call a parent and share their concern for their student in this manner. Something was going on and I feared what I might find out. Maybe I'd rather live in denial, than know the truth.

There were a few times that I had caught her smoking a cigarette on the front porch swing. She denied smoking when I asked her about it. "Really, I see the cigarette butt in the grass that you just threw over there when I came out the door." It was one of the many lies to come. It was obvious that she was apathetic. It was so sad to see her like this, because it was so out of character for her. She was usually so fun loving and spunky!

I remember a time she came home from shopping with inappropriate clothing for a 9th grader that she had bought at the mall. I told her to return them because she wasn't allowed to wear them. She became angry with me and told me that she liked them and she wasn't returning them!

Her brothers didn't want to be around her, because she was negative and snarky and just not fun anymore. They all had been close once and enjoyed one another, but it wasn't like this lately. It hurt my heart to watch all of this going on between my three children. There were so many things going on inside my head. I didn't know where to start or what to do!

It had been nearly three years since the earthquake of divorce hit our family. I was such a mess myself after learning about their dad's affair, which caused us to separate, and eventually divorce after nearly 17 years of marriage.

How does this happen to a Christian family that goes to church three times a week, reads Bible bedtime stories to the kids and who promised their children that they would never get divorced like their school friends' parents? I'm pretty sure that my kids were feeling some of the same feelings that I had, as little by little our seemingly 'perfect' world was destroyed. Where was the trust, honesty and especially faith that we preached to them? I imagine in our children's eyes their parents looked like hypocrites and liars. Everything that they'd been taught in their life was in shambles and destroyed, just as a tornado can so quickly demolish a house. So, what and who should they believe in now? How do they rebuild their lives after the devastation?

I was depressed and angry at what the divorce did to our family, and especially my kids! I was so wounded myself, I found it difficult to know what to do to help my three children cope after everything we'd known as a family was tossed away. Aimee desperately needed me and was trying to get my attention by acting out. I knew something wasn't right with her. I tried to talk to her, but she would tell me what I wanted to hear. She was such a sad girl! Her 'boo-boo' was just too big to kiss and make it all better this time! Help!

She continued down her road of self-destruction. One light in July, she snuck out of the house to go to a Pink Floyd concert, after she was told she couldn't attend, because of her negative behavior. Aimee was going to do what Aimee wanted to do. She had left a note on her bed that said,

"I'm very sorry + I love you guys, but I'm going to Pink Floyd. I've been waiting for many months. I am very sorry and I'll be back tomorrow. I love you." Aimee

I didn't know what else to do because I was scared, so I decided to call her Dad. I thought maybe we could figure something out together. Two heads are better than one, right? Although, it was easy for us to blame one other for her taking off and going to the concert.

We knew we had to wait until she would come back into town after the concert. We called around to some of her friends and eventually were told that some of the kids were staying at one of the boys' house.

It was after midnight, but we knew where he lived, so we went over there. We rang the doorbell, but no one answered. Then we saw kids darting back and forth in the house, so we knew someone was home. Why wouldn't they open the door? It was getting so frustrating!

Out of desperation, her dad called the police. A policeman showed up and he knocked on the door and called out through the door for someone to come out. But, no one did. Scenes like this were not a normal occurrence in our lives. Several months ago, Aimee was a dot your I's and cross your T's kind of person. This kind of behavior from her was so foreign to us. The policeman told us no law was being broken. She was willingly in the house, and didn't want to come out, and there wasn't anything he could legally do about it. This was not the news that I wanted to hear! "You're not serious, right? Make her come out! I wanted to get our daughter out of that house, so she could come home! But, no, we had to leave and wait until morning to hear from her. I felt utterly helpless and hopeless! I also felt like a terrible parent!

It was a long night of crying and calling out to God for help. I often wondered if He grew tired of hearing me whine. The past couple of years were very difficult. At times, I even wanted to throw in the towel, because the hurt was so intense. Eventually, she did call for a ride home. I think I jumped into the car quicker than I ever had before, to bring my Aimee home. I was upset with her, but, oh, how I loved her! I also knew she had to be hurting so much to be so disobedient. What had happened to my innocent daughter?

There was so much despair and darkness that it was hard to see where to take the next step. Which way led to the light? I knew that I'd been leaning more on my own human wisdom and strength than on Gods. It was obvious that I was in way over my head. Life was spiraling out of control. Aimee was so hurt and lost, and her Dad and I just weren't handling things well. Psalms 55:2 says, "Please listen and answer me, for I am overwhelmed by my troubles." I prayed earnestly that God would help her and give her new friends to help her find her way. This was the start of me learning to give God control. Aimee and I were both a mess! We needed God to show His power in our lives.

On September 13, 2000 Aimee told me that she had gone with her girlfriend to a meeting that helps teenagers with drug problems. She said that the counselor has asked her to bring her parents at the next meeting with her! Ohhh-Kaaay! It's strange that she's asking her Dad and me to go, instead of us begging her to go for help. But, we jumped on board in hopes that this was going to work for her.

I was scared to go. It was now confirmed that Aimee knew she had a drug problem. And now, I knew she had a serious enough problem that she needed help. It's tough facing the sad truth, but, I'm thankful that she saw it and was seeking help.

It was time for the parent meeting. Her Dad and I walked in united on Aimee's behalf. You can imagine my surprise when we walked in and I saw people that I knew. Thoughts ran through my head, 'Oh, so it was your son, and your daughter who did drugs with Aimee'. Sadly enough, having us all there was eye opening and yet, comforting. I wasn't alone in this battle.

That night, we agreed to enroll Aimee in the program. It would be an intensive 12 week outpatient program. She would be there every day working the program. It was a sad reality! But, I was thankful for this answer to my prayer.

When I drove Aimee there the next day, she begged me not to make her go inside. "I don't feel comfortable with them. They're not like me! Did you not see their face piercings, purple and pink hair and tattoos? We're too different! Please Mom." I reminded her that two of her friends dressed like her and that she had drugs in common with all of them. She reluctantly went inside. I promised to be back to pick her up. This was the beginning of a new road for her. It would be up to her to pave the way.

One night when I was going to pick her up it occurred to me that God had answered my prayers since she had new friends. When I realized this I began crying and thanking Him as I drove down Wilson Avenue. It sure wasn't what I would've picked, and I certainly didn't have a teenage drug rehab program in mind. But, "His ways are not our ways". Isaiah 55:8

The counselor mentioned that it was months of being

in the program before Aimee even started smiling. She said, "She looked dead inside". She wasn't working the program, so it was time to go to the next step. She was going to have to move to Denver to live with a family whose daughter had a year of sobriety. This crushed my heart! Aimee was very upset about moving. Her dad and I weren't happy with it either, but we wanted our daughter to be drug free. If she had to move out at age 16, then so be it! It was very difficult for all of us Never in a million years did I ever think my sweet, little, precious Aimee would have a drug problem and we would have to encourage her to move in with complete strangers. We were able to take her to the house and meet the parents and the family. It was with them and her being in Denver that she finally started working the program.

    I attended the weekly parent meetings in Denver, so I could also see Aimee each week. I wanted her to know that even at her lowest, and most difficult and darkest times, I loved her and was there for her. Eventually, I could see that she was getting back to her ole' sweet self.

    She also had to leave her high school and be homeschooled with the group. She graduated early and grew up fast. She gave up a lot with her choice to drink and do drugs. A soccer scholarship to college was now a dream of the past. There are consequences with the choices that we make in life.

    I can't help wondering what kind of parent people might think I was, if they knew that my teenage daughter had a drug problem. Often, I wanted to run and hide and not deal with people's judgments! I felt like I'd already had their eyes embedded in the back of my head the past two years, and now, there was Aimee to talk about. The despair of it all was overshadowed by her working the program, and becoming drug free. So overall, it was worth it! We had experienced the light of hope!

Looking back, I saw that I was concerned with how my life looked to people. It wasn't all wrapped up in a nice pretty bow! Oh, far from it! My box was crushed and the giftwrap was torn and the bow was frayed. But, you know what, there was still a surprise in the box...a gift was inside. It's such a fallacy today to think no one has problems or skeletons in their closets. We live in a fallen world after all, and we're all sinners. But, Jesus died on the cross for all of us and He can wipe our sins away if we choose to obey and follow Him.

We went through much hurt and sadness to get to a better destination. The alternative would've been so much more horrific! Aimee told me she would've been dead had she not entered the 3-year program. She said the program saved her life! A number of her friends couldn't quit doing drugs. Unfortunately, even at her young age, she's gone to many of her friends' funerals that had overdosed. It's too real and heartbreaking!

We all make choices in life and we have to deal with the consequences, whether they're good or bad. Aimee made choices based on her parent's decision to divorce. She decided to use alcohol and drugs to numb the extreme pain that she couldn't handle. She thought they were her answer, but it only took her further into a deeper, darker pit. The choices and decisions we make have a ripple effect that can either help or hurt others. Satan does a good job of discouraging us and deceiving us! He wants us to believe his lies. With God on our side, we're OVERCOMER'S! We win! What a gift!

After three years of working the drug rehab program Aimee graduated. I was so proud of her! She had the opportunity to use her bad and negative choices to share with middle school students about the danger of drugs and alcohol.

I learned a lot walking with Aimee on her drug free journey! Just because a kid has tattoos and piercings, or purple, pink or green hair doesn't mean there's something wrong with him. I think they've found something they can have control over in their life, because too many things are chosen for them by their parents. I know the kids from the program that visited in my home were kind and respectful people and I grew to care about each one of them. I've learned not to judge a book by its cover. Those days were some of the hardest that I've ever gone through, but I saw God at work and he made a better person out of me through the process. I've learned that it's better to have God leading the way. Psalms 41:10 "Don't' be afraid, for I am with you. Don't be dismayed, for I am your God. I will strengthen you. I will help you. I will uphold you with my victorious right hand." You don't have to go through your struggles alone. Give Him a call….He's waiting.

Contact Information
Anna Schmidt

At this writing Anna is in the final stages of writing "Our Scars of Hope" -- A soon to be released book filled with wonderfully, powerful stories to help you in your battles.

"Our Scars of Hope"
Available through Amazon,
Barnes and Noble, Books-A-Million,
and wherever fine Christian books are sold.

Carol Graham
Return the child. Give him back.

Although I was convinced I would have my own child one day, we decided to adopt a baby boy. We poured our love and our hearts into him as most parents would. A year had passed since we adopted Seth. When the phone rang that day, I had no reason to suspect anything unusual. My husband answered; and as I watched the expression on his face change rapidly, I did not like what I was observing. He called me over to share the receiver.

"I am getting pressure from my parents to raise my son so I am going to have to get him back. I am prepared to hire an attorney and you know you will not win."

Return the child. Give him back.
Carol Graham

At some point in our lives, each of us has probably been a victim, a victor, or both. The definition of victor is: One who defeats an adversary; the winner in a fight, battle, contest, or struggle.

The definition of victim is: One who is deceived or cheated, by his or her own emotions or ignorance, or by the dishonesty of others.

Like many other people, I was cheated, abused, hurt, and taken advantage of by others. I knew it was essential that I determine not to allow my emotions to overrule my intelligence. When I was bombarded with negativity, I had to choose how I would respond. A wise man once told me "When you buy the thought, you buy the lie!" I learned to say NO to negative thoughts, to defeatist ideas, to martyr attitudes. The more I resisted the thoughts, the easier it got.

Each time I had a major trauma in my life, I learned a serious life lesson. With each lesson is a story and each story brings hope to those who read it. So much of my life was shrouded in darkness and no amount of hope in the future could change the past.

There were many times I wanted to find a reset button but the only thing I could do was take one moment at a time, put one foot in front of the other, try to maintain a good attitude and never ever give up hope.

There were many losses in my life. I lost two children. I was kidnapped, raped, and left for dead by my abusive first husband. My current husband and I had two businesses stolen from us by corrupt partners who left us penniless and my husband was sent to prison when they lied and screamed fraud. This is the short list, but you get the idea. Life can be difficult but how we handle it determines who we become.

I was born with health issues that were often debilitating and caused me to wonder if my life would be cut short by disease. I watched my mother suffer my entire life and before my eighteenth birthday I said goodbye to her, for the last time.

I lived in constant pain as a result of endometriosis that was so severe I hemorrhaged three weeks out of any given month. I saw several gynecological specialists but there were no answers. I already had three surgeries to remove the endometrial tissue but it grew back almost immediately. Then I got the phone call from a gynecologist's office informing me he had a diagnosis. That conversation changed my life. There is one word in any language that is difficult to hear. That word is -- cancer.

It rolled off the doctor's tongue far too easily. I could not form my lips to mutter it. I was a young woman in my twenties. I was trembling and frightened.

"Carol, basically you have two choices and I think it is obvious which one you will choose!" I assumed he meant two types of treatment. He continued, "Your choices are hysterectomy or death." He paused for impact. "You are a very sick young woman." He seemed far too nonchalant about the whole matter.

Strength I did not know I had welled up inside of me and I said "I do not accept those choices. There has to be another way! I will find that alternative."

Rage overcame him. I had challenged his expertise. He rose up from behind his desk, leaned towards me and pointed his finger in my face. He was so angry he was shooting spit when he said, "Well then, lady, go home, suffer and…die!"

I stood up, spun on my heel and started out of the room. Then I paused, turned and said in a loud staccato voice, enunciating each syllable clearly. "I... will.... walk.... in here.... pregnant.... one day." I couldn't believe the words that came out of nowhere. But in my heart I knew I was going to succeed. Nothing was going to stop me. I almost screamed out loud "ENOUGH! Hysterectomy – I don't think so. Death? Not my time yet."

There was a seed planted in my heart as a little girl and the more I nurtured it, the stronger it became. My father told me I could feed my fears or feed my faith. The choice was mine.

What the doctor did not know was I had already lived decades of trauma. This was just one more battle to win, one more opportunity to be a victor and I really wanted to prove him wrong.

But, I had no idea what I was going to do. Thoughts of an agonizing death attacked me. But the Lord gave me a verse that I used in my thanksgiving prayer every single day. I put it on sticky notes all over the house. Whenever I had a negative thought or the pain was too intense to bear, I would pray that verse and remind my Heavenly Father of His promise to me. "And blessed is she who believed: for there shall be a performance of those things which were told her from the Lord." Luke 1:45 (KJV)

For 14 years, I held onto that verse. I never stopped thanking God for his promise to me. I praised Him for the baby I would hold in my arms one day. The battle never ceased but I grew stronger every day because I knew God's Word never returns void. I learned how to pray the answer, INSTEAD of the problem.

Although I was convinced I would have my own child one day, we decided to adopt a baby boy. We poured our love and our hearts into him as most parents would. A year had passed since we adopted Seth. When the phone rang that day, I had no reason to suspect anything unusual. My husband answered; and as I watched the expression on his face change rapidly, I did not like what I was observing. He called me over to share the receiver.

"I am getting pressure from my parents to raise my son so I am going to have to get him back. I am prepared to hire an attorney and you know you will not win." The words had been rehearsed and seemed too easy for her to say. A couple sentences, that's all it was -- a couple sentences that tore our hearts out.

"I'm afraid you don't really have a choice," our lawyer informed us. The law was clear. If we chose to fight, there would only be more agony and great expense. "I will set it up for you to return the child as soon as possible."

RETURN THE CHILD as soon as possible. I screamed on the inside. I cried on the outside. No, this just can't be happening. We loved Seth. He was ours. The bottom of my world dropped out from under me. I loved him and cared for him. He was part of our family for a whole year. I could not imagine life without him. I was his mommy. How could she do this to us? How could she possibly love him like we did? What about Seth? He would be torn from his parents, his home. Surely, he would feel the rejection. What path would his life take now? Nothing prepared me for the pain of relinquishing my son to someone who had not wanted him! But we had no choice. "Return the child. Give him back."

I watched from a distance as my husband handed him to her. It was in slow motion. I watched his hands leave the child as he lifted our son into her arms. He was handing our son to a stranger. I wanted to run and grab him but I was glued to the floor. I felt petrified. I thought I was either going to faint or throw up. My hand fluttered to my mouth for a moment fearing I might scream out. How could I go on? Where would I get the strength? This just could not be happening. Please God -- let this only be a dream. Tomorrow I will wake up and everything will be normal again.

When someone says it feels like their heart was in their throat that is accurate. My heart became so heavy it felt like there wasn't room in my chest cavity to hold it. The heaviness moved to my throat and even my extremities, weakening my entire body. I was fearful that my heart would implode, exploding on the inside from pressure, and yet wondered if that would bring some relief to the overwhelming state of heartbreak. My loss consumed my thoughts. Even when I was not thinking about it specifically, something would trigger a memory and the initial impact was felt once again.

In the months that followed, every time I saw a new baby or watched a child playing, I would cry. I could not go down the aisle in the grocery store that sold baby food without breaking down. Every time the telephone rang, I was hoping it was that 'woman' saying she had changed her mind. Days turned into weeks, then months........ then years. That was over forty years ago. I'll never forget our little boy.

Then it happened. I was pregnant -- just as God had promised. But my faith was put to a new test.

My pregnancy was 'touch and go' from the beginning. This pregnancy brought many complications and I spent most of it in a hospital bed. At least three times a week, the doctors would visit me in my room and be the bearer of more bad news.

"Carol, we have a new complication. Remember that this is a high-risk pregnancy and there is a strong possibility your baby will not make it. I want you to visit the nursery of premature babies once a week. This will help prepare you for what is coming. If your baby does survive he/she will not be normal and probably weigh a pound or two, at best. You can be sure of that!"

But God had a different plan! "V is for Victory!" That is what the doctor said when my daughter was delivered, just as God had promised. "You got what you wanted!" All I ever wanted was a baby and I was not sure what the doctor meant. Did he think I might give birth to something other than a baby? My five-year-old adopted son looked at his baby sister and said, "Mommy, I don't think she's cooked yet. She is all purple and shriveled and stuff!" I had to agree.

When the doc showed her to me I noticed a birthmark on her forehead in the shape of a "V." Rochelle was born SIX WEEKS EARLY; 6.6 pounds and her Apgar score was a perfect TEN. She is now the mom of my two grandchildren.

I have been married to the same man for 45 years. When asked what has kept our marriage together, my answer is "I keep him laughing." These 45 years included six years when he was bedridden, having suffered brain damage as a result of a car accident. But no matter what we endure, we can find humor to mute the pain.

I remember the first time I heard these words. It was unexpected. "Your husband has irreversible brain damage."

In 1995 my husband was in a car accident. The other driver didn't see him and hit him head-on. That day our lives changed forever.

Although Paul was in a lot of head pain, we assumed it would pass...soon. It didn't. Weeks turned into months and no number of medical tests could determine what had happened. Finally, an MRI showed that the seat belt Paul was wearing had cut into his neck sending a blood clot to his brain and solidified in an area that was inoperable, the Basal Ganglia. He suffered a stroke and started showing signs of Parkinson's disease. Things were escalating downward. Quickly.

He was hospitalized in an effort to regulate his medication but to no avail. The department head from the Psychology Department called me specifically to say that there was nothing they could do. The damage to his brain caused nerve damage throughout his body. He also applauded me for 'staying' with Paul. Apparently, most of these scenarios end in divorce. He had counseled Paul that he should expect this and not to hold it against me if I chose to leave him.

This was not even in my realm of possibility as I took an oath that said "in sickness and in health." What if I had been in accident? Life does not come with any warranties.

As those months turned into years, we had gained little ground. He vacillated between being a vegetable who could not feed himself to a raving maniac; a condition caused by various medication cocktails.

One of his diagnoses is Chronic Pain Syndrome (CPS). CPS is a condition when the brain tells the body that it is in pain but in reality, it is not. Consequently, pain medications do not work. Narcotics do not work. "Sorry," the doctors would say after each visit "but there is nothing we can do. This is as good as it is going to get."

The pain he endures is not a normal migraine. On a pain scale of one to ten - his number is off the charts. I do not know how he can open his eyes or function on any level.

After seven years, I said "Enough!" I have been a health coach/nutritionist for many years and knew if he was going to get help, natural medicine and prayer was his only hope. Replacing all his drugs with food supplements was no easy transition. There were some terrible withdrawal symptoms, lots of tears and discouragement but slowly, we started to see improvement. It is gradual but it is definitely happening. Patience is a new word in my vocabulary.

My heart always goes out to the spouses and families of those who suffer. It is extremely difficult to watch someone you love endure so much and know there is little you can do to make it better. That doesn't mean I don't have my share of pity parties. Fortunately, I don't stay there for very long.

Then reality slaps me in the face and I know there are better days ahead. It will get better. Things will continue to improve. We will get our lives 'back' again. I don't have to look very far to see scores of others who live in much worse situations. We are grateful for every single day.

One of the greatest lessons I have learned through adversity is to praise God from whom all blessings flow. No matter how difficult the situation, I can find something to thank and praise our Heavenly Father for within the situation. Not only does this change my perspective but it brings joy. Knowing that my steps are ordered by the God of the universe is beyond comprehension. God knows. God cares.

No, it isn't always easy to laugh but I cry my tears in private. Seeing ourselves as winners and focusing on finding a solution is a lot healthier than concentrating on everything that is going wrong. Sharing laughs with people around you is healing for everyone.

Finding humor in every situation may not be easy but it certainly helps you to survive. It will help you to maintain the attitude that you are a WINNER and not a loser. It keeps things in perspective.

One definition of success is: "Getting up one more time after you have been knocked down many times." Never stop getting up. Success is within our reach. But if we don't try, we become the victim. Fight the battle - become the victor.

I have been a victim of many circumstances but this is not where I live. I live in victory because I choose to live there. We certainly cannot control the things that may happen to us, but we can control where we live – in victory…or not.

Contact Information
Carol Graham

At this writingCarol is an Award winning Author of writing "Battered Hope" -- Carol is a resilient woman who endured traumatic events that would cause most others to roll over and quit. The challenges of cancer, rape, marital abuse, jail, loss of child and financial ruin coupled with a determination to succeed.

"Battered Hope"
Available through Amazon,
Barnes and Noble, Books-A-Million,
and wherever fine Christian books are sold.

Joy Wright Yarborough
The Wounds Of Love
Loves Isn't Selfish

I'm trying to find my son, who I haven't seen or talked to in 19 years. It's not like I didn't want him, and I never hurt or neglected him either. But sometimes circumstances unfold, and don't reflect the truth but instead protect mistakes. The story doesn't even matter anymore, people believe whatever they want, but the result was that I gave up my son at 4 so he could have a normal childhood and not be as damaged as I am, forever feeling abandoned and unwanted.

I died inside for about 2 years. I was completely and utterly depressed to the core of my being. I lost about 30 pounds in the first months, I quit a good job that I had, lost my apartment, and just died for awhile. I don't remember a lot about that time, I was only 21 and had literally lost everything that mattered to me. The worst part was how my mom totally DID neglect and mentally abuse me, and no one took me. I loved and tried and fought for my kids and lost them.

Loves Isn't Selfish
Joy Wright Yarborough

Nothing in my life has ever really been 'normal', so I'm not sure where to start. I have trouble believing my own story at times, but I have no reason to lie and tend to downplay things as opposed to exaggerate. I hope to be able to share my story more completely than I do normally. It's much more obvious that God has a plan for me when you get the full picture, instead of the watered down version I give to explain why certain things get to me.

I joke that God thinks I'm superwoman, because people always say that God doesn't give you more than you can handle. That statement used to make me mad, I saw others who seemed to be overwhelmed by stuff that I don't remember not knowing. But now I see it as something special, building up a lifetime of experiences that I can use to help others. God made me strong.

He shows me still that I am capable, and I may struggle moment to moment sometimes but I always seem to make it to the next thing. After awhile it's almost funny how much happens at once, but it's not exaggeration at all.

I grew up very differently, so it's hard for most people to realize that I don't see the world they do. I am ok with that, but it makes it hard to explain things if someone thinks if I don't fit their ideas then I'm lying.

I am a walking contradiction, and I have come to

enjoy it instead of feel shame. So with that in mind, I hope to help others with my openness to different.

I grew up having to adapt constantly. My mom would take off and leave me with different people all the time, and constantly weird circumstances. I also have congenital nystagmus, so I have bad vision and hearing. Two ear surgeries, eye patches and almost went blind and deaf before kindergarten. As well as a major sensitivity to the sun, growing up waiting for the shade to come out. Spent an entire summer bedridden and 3rd degree burns from a few hours in the sun around 6, so another unusual difficulty that I've known my whole life.

I lived with too many people to count, but nobody ever fought to keep me or call dhs. I lived with my grandparents a couple years, the only stable period in my childhood, refusing to speak to my mother for 2 yrs after she left me at my uncle's house to stay the night and didn't come back . After months she had to be notified via newspaper ad so my grandparents could get guardianship and enroll me in school. I moved back at 14 because it was too hard to deal with my grandparents thinking that I could just magically be normal. I moved back to my mom, because I was used to crazy at least. She was never a mother to me though, she was severely mentally abusive, neglectful, and put me through hell. She would leave me alone for weeks to take care of my sister with no food at 8. I had been kidnapped at 4. I had a very high I.Q., taking my first I.Q. test and was almost advanced a grade (by end of first grade I believe). I would think of answers that were correct but completely different in school, and always made honor roll and advanced classes even though I never actually tried. I would have no electricity or water at home, and still be able to find mistakes in text books and brought home stacks of awards. I always took care of my sister, but was told that I was a burden and to not bother anyone. I had ringworm go thru my bloodstream, leaving white spots that took years to fade. Once I had to listen to my mother get raped, and then she left us there. I called my sister's dad, he came and got her but no one came to get me for maybe a month or longer. When I moved back, I lost $75 dollars I had earned myself on the plane, they lost my luggage, and no one was there to pick me up at the airport (because my mom had been arrested for prostitution I found out later)

That was a pretty good indicator that I had made a bad decision, as I've had similar obvious signs at other significant times in my life too. In the time before I ran away, think I lived with 10 people.

I got woken up one time at 3 a.m. by police thinking my mom had killed a woman who died in our living room. I was used to weird stuff happening, she was a schitzophrenic drug addict, so I was mostly just annoyed that they had woke me up.

I ran away 6 months after I moved back, at 14. I was innocent as far as dating so I didn't realize that guys could be abusive and controlling. My first boyfriend was a psycho, it took me til I was 18 to get away from him. He would rape me, threaten to kill me if I left him, and scare anyone who tried to help me. But I could handle the physical easier than the mental. I am pretty mellow, so I didn't make him mad as long as I didn't leave. I got pregnant at 16, and turned myself in (runaway) so I could get healthcare. I was in a group home, which was fine. I was alone for his birth except for the last hour his dad showed up. My mom didn't. I was supposed to go home when he turned 6 wks.

We visited when he was 4 wks. 2 weeks later when I was able to get out of the home, my mom had moved. It took me a year to find her.

I am a natural mother, I love children. Eric was the first person who loved me unconditionally. I was finally happy. I was young, but never had trouble handling him. I didn't get mad and spank him, I always babysat or something to get what he needed. He knew his abcs before he could talk. And I never left him alone with anyone, I was very protective.

I stood up to his dad and broke a frying pan over his head when I first turned 18 to protect him. I had a protective order on him and I was terrified of his dad. I have never been aggressive or a fighter, but I was fearless when it came to protecting my son. His dad went to prison, and I finally got away from him for good. I had met a neighbor, my now first ex husband, and he helped me a lot. He was my first love. We went to stay at his dad's, out in the country, until we could get a place. We'd both been on our own awhile so it wasn't going to take long. He was 6 months younger, still 17 and I was 18. I think it was 3 months since Mark went to prison, and we had applied at a few apartments, but there weren't a bunch around out in the country. Mike, my bf then, has a younger brother who was always getting in trouble. July 29th, 1995, his brother stole a car and drove to his dad's in the middle of the night. He didn't live there. I woke up to cops everywhere, looking for stuff he had hidden from the vehicle around the property. I was asleep when he got there, I had no idea what was going on. They arrested me because I was over 18. I can't drive and I've never been a thief, but I was arrested for helping steal a car. They knew I wasn't involved, the cop told me he was going to arrest me and take Eric if I didn't tell him where everything was. I didn't know and was scared. I froze and couldn't talk, so I got arrested. I was in jail 3 days before they dropped my charges, and no one in my family would keep him. I told them no way he could go to my mom or his dad's family so they put him in emergency dhs custody. I literally walked from that courtroom, to the next and was released. They knew I was being released, they didn't even handcuff me. But with him in emergency dhs custody, I was told they had to do some paperwork and I would have him home. They said that for 3 months. Emergency custody is usually only 3 days to I have seen some states up to 30 days, but not 3 months.

On October 26, 1995 they put Eric in dhs custody. 3 days later on October 29th, my mother passed away. At the time it was ruled accidental overdose, but I have reason to believe now that her boyfriend had killed her for a $30,000 settlement she had just won. Her boyfriend never came to her funeral, recently I found that he has been involved in a murder for hire case, and her money was gone with nothing to show for it whatsoever. So it was pretty crazy circumstances, she was only 38. I was very angry with my mom when she died, years of mental abuse, and so it was very conflicting for me when she died so suddenly. I had actually seen her on the 26th, right after I had lost custody of Eric. I was only in town for a few days, so I left the address I was staying at. If I hadn't, I might have not known for awhile.

It was devastating, I had only recently gotten out of a very controlling, abusive relationship with Eric's dad, I had lost custody of my son for something I was innocent of, and my mom died 3 days later. Also, my best friend Jon had unexpectedly moved away. We had made plans to do something while I was in town, and his family sold their house so I didn't have him to talk to either. I thought I was going to lose my mind.

Their grounds for keeping Eric was they claimed neglect. When they had arrested me, I had been feeding Eric breakfast. Almost 2 year olds get very messy when they eat, so he was dirty from eating. He was the kind of child who didn't like to be dirty, if he took a drink and got water on his clothes he wanted to change. He got a bath every night, and cleaned up after every meal or snack or anything. But they arrested me while he was still in his high chair. And as many kids do, he had gotten head lice from some of the kids I babysat. I had just treated his hair the night before, but especially with vision problems, it takes more than one treatment to get rid of sometimes. But I had told them that he needed a treatment, it hadn't gone untreated. The box for the shampoo was still in the trash can. Neglect at that time was determined in the eyes of the caseworker. I think now they have actual guidelines.

They put Eric in a foster home, and I did everything they told me to plus some. I went through 3 years of court, so forgive me if this is mixed up in retelling my story. I had to go to court usually once every month. We had been living with Mike's dad, out in the country, so I moved back to the city I'm from. They broke many laws during the whole thing. At one point, I had written out everything for my attorney. It was 3 pages on college ruled paper of things they had done that violated the laws in my state. They refused to transfer the case to the county I lived in, and all of us had moved within the first few months. The caseworkers here petitioned multiple times to move the case here, it was ridiculous to have to find a ride 45 minutes away, knowing I can't drive, once a week for visitation, when no one lived in that county anymore.

The judge was also involved in cases with Mike's younger brother, who had been in trouble a lot. That alone is conflict of interest, and we shouldn't have had the same judge, she was biased against Mike's family, even though me and Mike had clean records. She even started talking to Mike during one of my hearings about his brother, which was another major violation.

My best friend Jon, who has now passed, had moved to the same small town that I had my court case in. He wound up working with the foster dad, and nobody knew this. He saw Eric with him one day and realized who they were. He informed me that they were a well established family in that town, and their family owned the trash company for that county. The foster mother at the time thought that she couldn't have children. They wanted to adopt Eric.

The judge violated my protective order on Eric's dad, scheduling our visitations to where we were both in the same place at the same time. She would move visits last minute to make it to where I was late, then it was counted against me for being late. Eric's dad failed a drug test, and I passed mine, and I had to attend meetings for 2 years once a week because they mixed us up. The court reports were inaccurate more than they were correct, and they usually left out the reports from the caseworkers in the city I actually lived. These caseworkers actually saw me more often, and included statements from the various classes, therapists, etc. that had been involved in the case. The reports from all of them were very strongly in my favor.

I had an attorney take my case for free, because of all the evidence she felt strongly I was being taken advantage of. She had told me that I was an easy target. My son was well behaved and well adapted, I didn't have any family support, I was young and didn't know all my rights, and I didn't have the money to fight them. I also had a C.A.S.A. worker quit when she was put on our case, and she tried to help us. C.A.S.A. is the court appointed child advocate.

Mike and I had a child, my daughter, and we got married. We got Eric back when my daughter was maybe a few months old. We had finished all of our parenting classes and whatnot several months before this. Eric came home right around the time the foster mother had finally had a child of her own. They gave the foster family visitation rights.

We had all been out of the small town now for over 2 ½ years, and had gone through counseling, parenting classes, play therapy, family workers, a bunch of stuff. I had people from my city in my home usually 3 days a week. My family had nothing to do with me because they believed I had done what I was accused of.

Mike and I were young, and it had taken a huge toll on our marriage. We split up. I had a new caseworker from the town my case was in show up, and I didn't know she was coming. I hadn't been feeling well, I had the flu or something, and I was taking a nap while my daughter was. Eric was watching a cartoon, and if you've ever been sick with kids you know that you wake up very easily when you have a preschooler. He was a very mellow child.

The caseworker, who had never been to my apt before, rang the doorbell and woke us up. My daughter had been asleep, and wet her diaper while sleeping. She woke up when I woke up from the doorbell. I had a 4 year old, and a one year old and there was a normal daily mess. I had a bag of trashed tied up but next to the trash can (I lived upstairs), toys in my living room floor, and a few dishes in my sink from breakfast and lunch. It wasn't a sinkful, just a few bowls and cups. I had court on February 25th, 1998.

It should have been my final hearing for all of this, and the caseworker who had only been to my house one time, told the judge that I seemed drugged and out of it when I had answered the door (I was sick and had just woke up), that my daughter was wet and crying (she had woke her up with the doorbell), and I had toys strewn across my house. What home with small children doesn't have toys everywhere? Then she brought up my lack of family support, something I have no control over. They took Eric from me again, and my daughter too.

Mike's grandparents got guardianship of my daughter, and they attempted to get Eric but the court wouldn't let them. His grandfather was a preacher, they had been foster parents before, and met all the requirements, and still had to hire an attorney to get my daughter. Before they got her, both kids were with the original foster home.

By this time, I pretty much broke. It was particularly hard on my son, who had already been taken from me before, and I couldn't let him go through any more. I tried to keep fighting for awhile, but I had a visitation and Eric gave me a big hug, and then told me he didn't want to come to my house. He even pushed his sister away. I have always had attachment issues, from my own childhood, and I recognized what was happening to him. He was about to start school, and I didn't want him to have the same problems I had. By this time we had been fighting the court 3 years, I had lost my mom, my family, my marriage, and I was alone. I was worn out. They weren't going to leave us alone, and I couldn't let him be pulled in different directions, so I gave up my rights. I did so out of love, because love isn't selfish, but it was the hardest thing I ever did. They jumped on it, had an emergency court hearing the same or next day (I can't remember very well, I got very depressed after this) to terminate my rights. My daughter was with her grandparents, who had guardianship, so it was finally over.

I died inside for about 2 years. I was completely and utterly depressed to the core of my being. I lost about 30 pounds in the first months, I quit a good job that I had, lost my apartment, and just died for awhile. I don't remember a lot about that time, I was only 21 and had literally lost everything that mattered to me. The worst part was how my mom totally DID neglect and mentally abuse me, and no one took me. I loved and tried and fought for my kids and lost them. The worst kind of oxymoron ever.

In the last few years, I've found that 4 different people involved in my case have either been fired or stepped down. They have had other people come forward saying the same things as me. They wouldn't return kids after the parents fulfilled the courts wishes. They told potential foster parents that they would be able to adopt. They accepted bribes from county utilities and agencies. The judge and district attorney have both had such complaints, along with some of the caseworkers whose names I can remember. There's actually much more than I've mentioned, but you get the idea.

I learned a very harsh truth: true freedom comes from losing everything. When there's nothing left to lose, there's nothing left to fear. I wasn't afraid of death, and to be honest I wanted to die for several years. I was suicidal for awhile, but God wouldn't let me die. He wasn't done with me yet. I got very sick a few times, but had divine intervention.

Eventually I had 2 more children, got married and divorced again, and got back on my feet. I got to see my older daughter, and later her grandparents let her come live with me. She is now almost 21. I suffered with depression most of my life, but I also found that I was really good at talking to people. I had lost so much, there wasn't a whole lot that I couldn't understand so people still tend to come to me when things are bad. I've had many people tell me things they've never told anyone else, and I enjoy being able to help someone else get through the tough times.

As I said, I had divine intervention. When my second daughter was little, and my son was a baby, I had a very strange case of appendicitis. My older daughter was 6 I believe. She had come to visit, and I couldn't get up to play with her. I had lived with depression for a long time, so I tended to ignore my body, but when I couldn't get up and play with my daughter (she was a lot more active than my younger daughter) I knew something wasn't right. My older daughter also out of the blue came up to me and told me she didn't want me to die. A very strange thing for a 6 year old to say.

About a week after she left, I went to check my mail, and I had an insurance card in the mail. The same insurance my kids had, but I wasn't on it before. Ok God, I'm listening. I went to the hospital, and they noticed I had been there maybe 3 or 4 times in 6 months with the same complaint. They had done a few tests but didn't know what was wrong. I had some type of scan, and it showed up I had calcium deposits (stones) and they thought maybe I had crohn's disease. More tests, 2 more months of doctor visits, a few specialists, and I finally had to have exploratory surgery because they didn't know what was wrong with me. I was throwing up constantly, couldn't eat, gaining weight, and in constant pain.

I was in the hospital 8 days. I was cut from above my belly button to my bikini line, about 24 staples. A big incision for appendicitis. The doctors said that I had multiple perforations on my appendix but it was healing itself, and I had stones in my appendix. Somehow I had appendicitis and a ruptured appendix more than 6 months and it didn't kill me. My nurse said in 25 years she had never heard of a case like mine.

I've actually had a few other stories of divine intervention just as spectacular and undeniable. When I gave birth to my younger son, I was induced. I had a hard labor, with a few complications on my end and was in the hospital for about a week. I had my tubes tied afterwards, and when they went in they found that I had internal bleeding. Another time I had split up with my 2nd ex husband, and the next day got a phone call at home offering me a job. It was a very good job, and I hadn't been looking for a job and hadn't worked in about a year because of my daughter being so young. I even worked there for a few weeks not knowing how much I made because I enjoyed it so much.

With so many obvious things in my life showing that God had a plan, I started to see myself in a better light. I saw that I could help others and I am happy doing it. I want to be a counselor of some kind eventually, but I joke that I'm already an unofficial therapist. I have put in many, many hours talking with people during their darkest hours, and there are times that I've told people stuff that later they came to me and said that God was speaking to them. It wasn't anything that was from me, it was something that would come to me in the moment that meant something to them specifically that they saw later. Its been a wonderful thing to find some good for all the bad. I have had lots of people say that I've understood them when no one else did, so that makes me happy to hear. I know that I've struggled to deal with everything, and even therapists didn't understand the massive weight I carried. So if I can lighten that load for anyone else I am happy to.

I have a great "adopted" family (not literally, just good people who I love and call my family) now who have helped me slowly heal. I have a lot of "adopted" kids now who call me mom, my younger 2 kids are happy and very good kids. My older daughter had moved to California with her dad for awhile after she turned 18.

No one can explain how it happened but the records pertaining to the adoption were either lost or misplaced. The state had lost track of my son. For years, every time I saw a boy the age of my son, my heart would cry out to God. "God, help me find my son." Every Christmas, every birthday, every thing sparked that cry, "God, help me find my son."

My story is not the same as other peoples stories. I asked that I be able to tell my story in this book – hoping that someone might help me find my son. The editor of this book said that I could. He said he could not promise me that my son would be found; but, he did say that <u>Romans 8:28 would win out in the end.</u>

As I was writing my story, Romans 8:28 worked things together for good. I found my older son. I had been looking for him for many years. I literally found him on social media about an hour before my daughter got home from being out of state the last few years. My son is now about to be 24. I haven't seen him yet, he lives out of state, but I found out that I have a one year old grandson too. My son grew up an only child (he was adopted by a different family, not the original foster home). He loved hearing that he had siblings, and found that they have a lot in common.

God works in mysterious ways, so don't give up no

matter how dim it may seem. I am definitely a testimony to that! God bless you all; and remember, God loves you and <u>Romans 8:28 will win out in the end</u>.

John Dee Jeffries
Chicken

A memory is like a footpath. It meanders backward and forward through time. Some memories are rooted in the past -- and we work our way backward to meet them. Other memories, even though they too are rooted in the past come near, traveling forward through time back to us, to greet us.

As we close this first volume of *Broken Beyond Belief -- But Not Beyond Faith* I remember and recall an earlier time. I was a young pastor visiting someone who lived on a farm. Behind the house was an open field and a large wooded area. At a fork in the trail that ran behind the farmhouse was a big red barn and a barnyard – and horses, cows, goats, pigs, and chickens.

If I sit still long enough I can still hear the sounds, see the sights and smell the pungent smells. The ground was like mush, covered with barnyard animal tracks. What I remember most, however, was the sudden flush of dark storm clouds and the rush of activity by barnyard animals as they scurried to escape the sudden downpour.

As the rain fell, harder and harder, the farmer and I, like barnyard animals, ran for cover. Finding shelter near a chicken house we paused and what I saw next was, well, unforgettable.

As the rain continued to fall, in the middle of the barnyard a mother hen was cackling, louder and louder, calling her little chicks to shelter under her extended wings. The little chicks were racing and running for cover under the extended wings of the mother hen, escaping the rain, and the winds that swirled around them.

One little chick, however, did not heed the momma hen's call. It just stood there – alone, cold, shivering in the cold rain.

In the Bible and in life, Jesus likens himself to a mother hen, with wide, safe wings outstretched for protection and shelter in the time of storm or trouble.

In Luke's Gospel Jesus said, "how often I have longed to gather you as a hen gathers her chicks under her wings -- but you were not willing."

Hey! Is that you out there, troubled and blown about by the rough winds of life? Shivering? Alone? Sooooo Not Necessary! Enough Said!

CERTITUDE
CLOSING COMMENTS
John Dee Jeffries

When the seas are rough, remember one thing -- they will get calm again. When the seas are calm, remember one thing -- they will get rough again. Know this: we all need a good ship to get us safely through both calm and rough seas. That ship is Jesus! He is the Captain of our Salvation!

The Bible promises this: tough times are temporal, temporary but God's love endures forever! So what does this mean to you? Just this: from time to time everybody faces hardships and disappointments – even disappointment with God – and so will you. When tough times arrive, God always stands ready to protect you and help you. Your task is straightforward – you must share your burdens with Him. (I don't know who you are, but I have a feeling I've written this a second time -- just for you…so, share your burdens with Him – now!)

What do you do when the bottom falls out? When the bubble breaks? When it looks as if your dreams are turning to ashes? Remember this: Keep on believing! You've not lost everything until you've lost your faith! And that's a choice – never an accident!

Somewhere near you, perhaps around the corner, perhaps down the street, God has a church filled with loving people led by a kind, wise, godly pastor. They're waiting for you and your family. Go there.

Do you feel as though you've lost your way? Are you tired of the "same ole – same ole" routine of life, the same old grind of life? Do words like -- Purpose! Plan! Providence! Design! Destiny! -- are these words foreign to your vocabulary?

And what of the promises of Jesus – the promise of abundant life? It's His promise – to you! -- and to me! To all who have received Him!

Perhaps it seems as if you're going in circles and don't know what to do. Today, perhaps more than any other time in history, people are dissatisfied with their lives.

Let me ask a question! Have you ever been in the car with someone who refuses to admit they're lost? It's frustrating. You realize they need to put pride aside and ask for directions. Well, life is much like that.

Ask for directions! God has an eternal Master Plan! No one can stop it! Many will miss it! You have a role to fulfill, a part to play, a destiny to fulfill!

Go for it! Seek, Shape then Share God's vision for your life. Run with patience the race that is before you!

In Christ -- I'm praying for you – John

BROKEN BEYOND BELIEF -- BUT NOT BEYOND FAITH

BROKEN BEYOND BELIEF -- *BUT NOT BEYOND FAITH*
FROM BROKENNESS TO BLESSEDNESS
Volume Two

Published By Parables is putting together Volume Two of *Broken Beyond Belief -- But Not Beyond Faith.* Its an incredible collection of true stories of twenty amazing people who were *Broken Beyond Belief – But Not Beyond Faith.* You may be one of the twenty or know of someone who should be. Contact us.

Published By Parables
2813 Regal Dr.
Chalmette, LA 70043

www.PublishedByParables.com

fbc.chalmette@gmail.com

Broken Beyond Belief -- But Not Beyond Faith

BROKEN BEYOND BELIEF -- BUT NOT BEYOND FAITH

www.ingramcontent.com/pod-product-compliance
Lightning Source LLC
Chambersburg PA
CBHW071729080526
44588CB00013B/1948